St Joseph Convent
Easton, Penn

BEARING
WITNESS

BEARING WITNESS

The Place of the Franciscan Family
in the Church
JEREMIAH CROSBY O.F.M. Cap.

FRANCISCAN HERALD PRESS
Publishers of Franciscan Literature
Chicago, Illinois 60609

BEARING WITNESS, The Place of the Franciscan Family in the Church, by Jeremiah Crosby O.F.M.Cap., Library of Congress Catalog Card Number: 65-16675, copyright 1966 by Franciscan Herald Press, 1434 West 51st Street, Chicago, Illinois 60609. Designed by Publication Associates. Made in the United States of America.

IMPRIMI POTEST:
Most Rev. Clementinus of Vlissingen
Minister General O.F.M.Cap.

CENSORES LIBRORUM:
Alexis Luzi O.F.M.Cap.
Jogues Constance O.F.M.Cap.

IMPRIMATUR:
Most Rev. Cletus F. O'Donnell, D.D.
Vicar General, Archdiocese of Chicago

November 19, 1965

TO
THE FRANCISCAN FAMILY
AND THE CROSBY FAMILY;
ESPECIALLY TO
THE MEMORY OF MY DAD

Preface

The papal court hummed with activity. The powerful Cardinal John of St. Paul stood before Pope Innocent III pleading the cause of a little brown-robed man of God. The man was Francis of Assisi. He had recently told the cardinal that he had been instructed by the Lord to go and rebuild his Church. "I have found a most excellent man," the cardinal said to the Holy Father, "who desires to live according to the form of the Gospel and in everything to observe evangelical perfection. I am convinced that through this man our Lord wills to renew the faith of Holy Church in the whole world."[1]

Later the Pope had a dream; the church of St. John Lateran was crumbling and about to fall. At the same moment a little man in the garb of a peasant came across the piazza to support it with his shoulders, saving it from collapse. The next day the great Pope recognized the man in the dream as the brown-robed Assisian who now stood before him. Though he sensed something special in this intense and vibrant youth standing before him, the Holy Father could not immediately approve the outline of life Francis had laid before him. Thus the Pope sent him away for a time, while he thought and prayed.

7

After a time Pope Innocent III approved the Franciscan rule. Later, blessing Francis and his followers he said, "Go with the Lord, brothers, and as the Lord will deign to inspire you, preach penance to all."[2]

Seven hundred and fifty years later, again in the Lateran, another great pope, John XXIII, sat upon the Chair of Peter. Commemorating the first approval of Francis' rule given by his powerful predecessor, Pope John noted:

> Here in the Basilica which is *'urbis et orbis mater et caput,'* it is not the apostles who bring us together this evening but St. Francis of Assisi, *'homo catholicus et totus apostolicus,'* who, through the span of seven centuries, gathers his sons about him. From the great bronze statue in this immense piazza he invites us to contemplate the magnificent and wonderful papal and partriarchal See . . . This evening, it is the monument commemorating his rule which has attracted our attention. One would say that the statue of Pope Innocent III of incomparable memory, who is reposing here in this noble and magnificent tomb, appears to have awakened from his rest in order to reassure us of the reality of his dream, the prodigy of divine Providence.[3]

These words of Pope John can be predicated of each one of the modern popes. Innocent III appears to have awakened from his rest in order to reassure the Vicars of Christ of the past century that, without doubt, his dream still continues. At the same time he is reassuring us Franciscans that we also can help support and revitalize the structure of the Church. The words of Pope John XXIII addressed to us are evidence of this fact.

Because of their constant appeal made to the Franciscan family to be instruments of reform in our age as Francis was in his, some may wonder aloud why the children of the Seraphic Man are not in the front ranks of the Church's renewal. The fact is, the Franciscan family aims to have not one or the other isolated friar, sister, or tertiary become involved in the renewal of society, but to have each of them personally committed to it as a necessity flowing from his or her vocation as a member of a family in the Mystical Body of Christ. The very term "vocation" implies the fact that we have been *called* to make a response. The response each of us must make is the same response Christ made to the Father, the same response Francis made to Christ, namely, that of bearing witness — showing the world the reality of the truth we believe in.

The dialogue of salvation thus has two aspects: the call or vocation and the response or witness. Today this is continued in the community of salvation, the Church. Our vocation and witness must take place in the community in which we have been called and through which we make our response. It must, therefore, mirror the total vocation and witness of the Church Itself.

This fact applies to the friars. It applies as well to the Poor Clares, for they exist in the Church not for themselves, but to promote the kingdom of God through their prayers[4] and even, as Pope Pius XII has particularly shown,[5] by limited apostolic activity. It applies to the Third Order religious, including the sisters, as Cardinal Suenens has shown so effectively. It applies no less to all tertiaries, who by their lives as Christians and their vocation as Franciscans are called to build up the Body of Christ in their own hearts and in the heart of the world.

The purpose of this book is to explain in synthesis how the modern popes since Leo XIII have outlined the pattern

upon which the Franciscan family can help accomplish
the renewal of society. So the purpose is not to write
of past or present failures and successes, but rather to indi-
cate what should be accomplished as declared by the
popes. The means that will be used to accomplish this task
can be found in the encyclical of Pope Paul VI, *Ecclesiam
Suam*. Since the Franciscan family is an organ in the Mystical Body, the needs Pope Paul outlined for the Church
must be the same for the Franciscan family. Today these
needs are threefold. First of all, there ought to be an awareness of the nature of the Franciscan family just as there
must be an awareness of the nature of the Church. Second
there must be continual renewal and reform. Finally, by
reforming ourselves we will be able to contribute our share
in the dialogue of salvation with the modern world.[6]

To understand what this awareness means to the Franciscan family, recall an important scene from the life of
our Seraphic Father. After Francis received his inspiration
to rebuild the Church of Christ, he said to his first disciples,
"I see, Brothers, that God in his mercy means to increase
our company; let us therefore go to our holy Mother the
Roman Church and lay before the supreme Pontiff what
our Lord has begun to work through us; so that with his
consent and direction we may continue what we have undertaken."[7]

From the very beginning, Francis was subject at the feet
of the Church. Towards the end of his life, as we know
from history, he turned the whole order over to the Church
completely to be guided by her.[8] In all things his order
was to reflect the image of the Church, it was to be totally
ecclesial.

We know to what an extent Francis was aware of the
role of his order in the Church when we recall the famous

dispute over studies. We all know his distrust of studies. He considered them of little value for himself or his friars. Yet, when the needs of the times demanded it and the popes ordered it, Francis *cheerfully* acceded and opened houses of studies — almost, it would seem, in direct antithesis to the perfection of his spirit and life. In reality, however, this was nothing but the synthesis or the perfection of his spirit and life, for his spirit was to act on the words of the vicars of Christ and his life was to live the life of the Church.

After showing that we become aware of the nature of the order in the Church by being subject to it for our spirit and life, we will show that this awareness expresses itself in penance, a life of reform. Then by showing how the popes interpret the continual reform which took place in the life of Francis and his apostolate, we will show how they apply the same elements of his interior life and apostolate to his twentieth-century sons and daughters. In this way the dialogue of salvation will be continued with and in our world.

The book is based on the major comments on the Franciscan spirit made by Popes Leo XIII to Paul VI. This includes three encyclicals as well as many other addresses and letters. Besides these, I have used materials from minor statements made expressly to the Franciscans and have also included references to other pronouncements made by them. In this way it is hoped the chapters, especially the ones in Part Three, *Reform and Dialogue with the World*, will express the spirit and life of institutes in the Church as the popes have interpreted.

I have tried to parallel the importance of themes found in the various chapters with the amount of stress given them by the popes. If in some cases there will be a lack of stress (or no stress) on certain subjects it does not mean they are not part of the Franciscan spirit. It merely indicates they were not stressed by the popes. Since Part Three of this book deals with the present-day situation, I have developed the thoughts of the popes and have commented on them to a greater extent here than in the other sections.

In certain places it may seem the popes emphasize points not usually stressed. It may also seem they over-stress particular points or stress things which may even appear alien to our spirit. If this seems to be the case, let us not jump to the conclusion they have been wrong. As Francis did regarding studies, let *us* rather look to our genuine spirit. If we do, we can only deduce that our life is to be lived at the feet of these popes, not only listening to their words of counsel for us, but eager to put them into practice.

Many times we read that a book has been written to fill a need. The same can be said of this book. More important than filling a need, however, it is hoped this book will *create* a need, the need for the whole Franciscan family to look to the official interpreters of our spirit and life in the Church. Reinforced in our age by the same authentic, paternal guide which strengthened Francis in his, may we bear witness in our lives to the same Gospel-image of the Church which Francis radiated in his own. Like him also, may we continually express this image of the Church to all God's People spread everywhere throughout the whole world.

Jeremiah Crosby O.F.M.Cap.

St. Anthony Friary
Marathon, Wisconsin

Acknowledgments

I would like to express my sincere thanks, first of all, to my fellow-friars at St. Anthony's Friary for their unfailing support during the writing and preparing of the manuscript for publication. Such people, we often read, are the ones "without whose help this book would not have been possible." In reality, this book probably would have been completed without the continued help of so many of my confreres. But it would not have been completed so soon, nor would it have been the community effort and pleasure that it turned out to be.

I would like to thank, in particular, my superiors — Most Reverend Clementinus of Vlissingen O.F.M. Cap., Minister General, and Very Reverend Gerard Hesse O.F.M. Cap., Minister Provincial, for permission to publish this book; Very Reverend Gerald Walker O.F.M. Cap., Ex-Minister Provincial and present Director of Clerics, who encouraged me from the first and helped the work with his prayers and guidance; Frs. Alexis Luzi and Jogues Constance O.F.M.Cap. who reviewed the manuscript and, along with the other priests, offered valuable insights and encouragement.

Special thanks are also due my brother, Fr. Nevin Crosby, and my other confreres, Frs. Venard Hemauer, Antonio Rios, Mitchell Kraft, Emmanuel Hagman, Dacian Markwell, Maurice Craig, Colman Kronzer, Kirk Koehler, Cosmas Hicks, Linus Bertram, and Rodney Reichling for the innumerable hours they spent in various aspects of preparing the manuscript for publication.

Finally I would like to thank Mr. William Bruce of the Bruce Publishing Company for his valuable information and all the other companies for graciously granting permission to use their material. Their names will appear in the various notes.

To all of these, then, I want to express my deepest gratitude and thanks. May the Lord give them his peace.

Contents

Abbreviations

AAS	— *Acta Apostolica Sedis,* Roma.
Acta Leonis	— *Acta Leonis XIII, Pontificis Maximi,* Roma.
AOFM	— *Acta Ordinis Fratrum Minorum,* Roma.
AOFMCap	— *Analecta Ordinis Fratrum Minorum Capucinorum,* Roma.
ASS	— *Acta Sanctae Sedis,* Roma.
Cel.	— Life of St. Francis by Brother Thomas of Celano
COFMConv	— *Commentarium Ordinis Fratrum Minorum Conventualium,* Roma.
Conf.	— Confraternity of Christian Doctrine translation of the Holy Bible (New York: Benziger Brothers, Inc., 1961).
Courtois	— *The States of Perfection:* Papal Documents from Leo XIII to Pius XII, ed. Abbe Gaston Courtois, trans. Rev. John A. O'Flynn (Westminster, Maryland: The Newman Press, 1961).

de Robeck	— The Legend of the Three Companions, *St. Francis of Assisi: His Holy Life and Love of Poverty*, trans. Nesta de Robeck (Chicago: Franciscan Herald Press, 1964).
FHF	— *Franciscan Herald and Forum*, Chicago.
Hermann	— *Saint Francis of Assisi*, Thomas of Celano, trans. Placid Hermann O.F.M. (Chicago: Franciscan Herald Press, 1963).
Husslein	— *Social Wellsprings* II, ed. Joseph Husslein S.J. (Milwaukee: The Bruce Publishing Company, 1949).
Leg. Maj.	— *Seraphici Doctoris S. Bonaventurae Legendae duae de Vita S. Francisci Seraphici* (Quaracchi, 1898).
LTC	— *Legend of the Three Companions.*
The Messenger	— *The Messenger* 12 (Detroit: St. Bonaventure Monastery, 1949).
OR	— *L' Osservatore Romano*, Citta del Vaticano.
Peruffo	— *Il Terz' Ordine Francescano nel Pensiero dei Papi*, ed. Ambrogio Peruffo O.F.M. (Roma: Commissariato Generale del T.O.F. dei Frati Minori, 1944).
RHS	— *Rome Hath Spoken* (Chicago: Franciscan Herald Press, 1958).
TPS	— *The Pope Speaks*, Washington D.C.
Walsh	— *The Mind of Paul VI*, ed. James Walsh S. J., trans. Archibald Colquhoun (Milwaukee: The Bruce Pub-

	lishing Company, 1964).
Words	— *The Words of Saint Francis,* an anthology compiled and arranged by James Meyer O.F.M. (Chicago: Franciscan Herald Press, 1952).

NOTE: The quotations from foreign languages are translated from the original sources. I have tried to remain faithful to existing translations. Where the complete translation are available, I have noted them.

All Old Testament scripture quotations are taken from the New Confraternity edition. They will not be noted. Except where noted, the New Testament scripture quotations are taken from *The New Testament in Modern English,* trans. J. B. Phillips (New York: The Macmillan Company, 1963).

Part One

AWARENESS OF THE NATURE OF FRANCISCANISM

Chapter One

"AT THE FEET OF THE SAME HOLY CHURCH"

Over thirty years ago, Pope Pius XI expressed the thoughts of millions who have lived during the past seven and one half centuries:

> Today you may hear it said that Christianity is in need of another Francis to reform it. But suppose in the wake of this revived enthusiasm, mankind would allow Francis to teach it the ways of piety and sanctity; suppose all men would follow in their own lives the example which he, 'the mirror of virtue, the way of righteousness, and the rule of conduct,' has left us; would that not be powerful enough in itself to heal and drive out the corruption of the times?[1]

Not very long ago, many began to believe that Christianity has been given another Francis to reform it, another mirror of Christ whose universal appeal has brought the world closer to the love of God and the observance of the Gospel message of penance and peace. He was Angelo Giuseppe Roncalli, the pope who "affectionately loved to say"[2] he had been a tertiary son of Francis for over sixty-five years. This man's reform mirrored the reform of Francis, just as Francis' reform mirrored the re-

form of Christ. It was a personal reform, a personal turning to God in love, as well as a personal turning to God's
people in active, practical charity. Such is the reform
this great son of our Seraphic Father showed the world
which waited for Francis to return again to earth. As
John Cogley wrote in *Commonweal:*

> For years we heard that the world needed another
> Francis of Assisi, a saint who by the sheer force of
> his personality and human qualities would dramatize
> the message of Christianity in modern times. We have
> not lacked saints in our generation. . . . But none of
> them, even among the canonized, has fulfilled what
> might be called St. Francis' special vocation, to be a
> saint whose appeal reached out to men everywhere.
> Those who looked for 'another St. Francis' had that
> rare quality in mind. . . . It does not seem an exag-
> geration, under these circumstances, to state that the
> 'new St. Francis' — the one so many prayed for over
> so many years — died on June 3, 1963. That the world
> recognized him, despite the fact that he was not a poor
> friar wandering over the face of the earth with an
> apocalyptic message but lived amid the splendor and
> formality of the Vatican, cheerfully occupying the
> most awesome office on earth, only adds to the wonder
> and paradox of Pope John's life. . . . Every Francis-like
> saint has a great message for his age. . . . He was a
> quiet, gentle revolutionary, this pope, whose dynamite
> — as might have been expected of another St. Francis
> — was faith, hope, and charity. . . . He accepted the
> world, not as the world might be, or as it should be,
> or even as it could be, but as it is — and he went on
> from there. Reality was ever his starting point. . . .

The pope did not change the world, but he came as close to doing so as any human agent could. If John XXIII was not the new St. Francis we looked for, what manner of man will such a saint be?[3]

The whole Franciscan order can and should rejoice in these words. Yet we may also ask, why was this "new St. Francis" Pope John? Why wasn't it one of the forty-five thousand members of the First Order, or one of the fifteen thousand members of the Second Order (St. Clare was one of the greatest imitators of St. Francis and social reformers in the history of the Church),[4] or another one of the more than two million members of the Third Order, religious and secular, or one of the more than ten thousand members of the Franciscan secular institutes?

The answer, of course, rests primarily on realizing the fact that God chooses whom he wills to accomplish his end in the world. That he chose someone in such an exalted position as Pope John is a matter of his providence. However, the answer may also lie in the fact that Pope John was one of the few Franciscans who truly understood the message of Francis.

For years the question has been asked by his followers, "What would Francis do if he were here today?" Pope John has given the answer to this question in his life, a living symbol of the appeal of the Franciscan ideal in the twentieth century.

Providentially, God chose a pope himself to put into practice the papal appeals made to the Franciscans to be for our age what Francis was for his. Perhaps now that such a timely model stands before us, the pleas of the Vicars of Christ will be more easily put into practice. Because John lived and loved it will be easier to put into

practice the ideals Francis would proclaim if he were
living today.

If Francis *were* living today, would not his order occu-
py a position in the front lines of the Church's *aggiornamento,* in Catholic Action, in liturgical reform, in scripture studies, in saving society? Would not the words
"Franciscan" or "Friar Minor" give a thrill to the heart
of the hearer once again as they did in 1226? Would not
the world look to us, followers of Francis, with expectant
hope that we might once again lead it to the correct living
of the dynamic Gospel message of reform — that message
of penance and peace which springs from love?

THE ROLE OF THE CHURCH

If Francis would live again today he would do what
he did while he was alive; he would go to the Church. Before his death, he turned the order completely over to
the Church to be the servant of her every wish and command,

> so that, submissive and subject always at the feet of
> the same holy Church, grounded in the Catholic faith
> (Col. 1, 23), we may, as we have firmly promised, ob-
> serve the poverty and the humility and the Holy
> Gospel of our Lord Jesus Christ.[5]

At the feet of the Church we become aware of our spirit
by listening to the words of the popes. At the feet of the
Church we live our life, the life of our Head, by partici-
pating in the Church's liturgy. Franciscan spirit cannot
survive unless it is vivified with the Spirit-guided words
of the community of Christ. Franciscan life cannot exist
unless it is lived in union with the life of that community,
the liturgy. These two elements, spirit given in the words

of the visible heads of the Church and life given by participation in her liturgical life, form the poles about which Franciscan spirit and life revolve.

"Religious orders have come into existence through the action of the Church, which gives the sanction of her authority"[6] to their way of life, Pope Leo XIII declared. The genius of Francis, through the Church, gave his order its peculiar spirit and life which was so spontaneous. The Church added to this the element of stable order through the vows, especially the vow of obedience. Francis gave the ideal of freedom to this obedience while the Church gave order to the spontaneous freedom through her norms. As Pope Leo noted: "Those who thus bind themselves by the obligation of vows, far from suffering the loss of liberty, in fact enjoy a much fuller and more noble freedom, the liberty with which Christ has made us free."[7]

The stability in the order and the spontaneity in the freedom which resulted in the great Franciscan reform movement can be expressed most clearly in one concept, peace; peace in the individual, peace in the Church, peace in society.

Such peace could never be achieved without the guidance of the Church. This is why Francis said:

> I will go, therefore, and I will commend them to the holy Roman Church, by the rod of whose power those of ill-will will be struck down and the children of God will enjoy full freedom everywhere unto the increase of eternal salvation.[8]

Franciscan Spirit
Determined by the Words of the Popes

The popes, as vicars of Christ, are the true heads of our order, just as Christ is the true Head of the Church. Thus,

for Francis and his first followers, the words of the popes
were words of fatherly counsel. The mind of the Church
gave the spirit and interpretation to the rule, which was
"the mirror of the Gospel." As the constitutions of the Friars Minor state so clearly:

> The obedience which the blessed Father Francis
> had learned by heavenly enlightenment, he himself
> showed, taught, and commended to be shown by all
> the members of his order to the Roman Pontiff, the
> supreme Vicar of Christ upon earth. All the friars, as
> meet and just, are therefore bound to show humble
> reverence, the greatest honor, and the most steadfast
> obedience and fidelity to His Holiness the pope and
> to the Holy Apostolic See. The superiors, moreover,
> should promote among their subjects the knowledge
> and enforcement of the decrees of the Holy See re-
> garding religious.[9]

Only by putting these words into practice have the sons
and daughters of Francis been successful in the Church.
It will be only by continuing to adhere to these words that
they will be in the Church what the popes desire. In his
address to the members of the First Order and Third Order Regular upon the 750th anniversary of the approval of
the rule, Pope John said:

> The history of the Church, when studied without ani-
> mosity, provides a very exhaustive documentation of
> two things: how, on the one hand, success adorns the
> life of religious orders when they preserve a pure and
> simple obedience to the Holy Church; and how, on
> the other hand, disadvantage and desolation, lament-
> ing and weeping, befall them when they pursue, either

alone or collectively, the paths of insubordination and lax discipline.[10]

The Franciscan family has always gloried in its obedience to the Holy See. The Holy See as well glories in our submissiveness to her. Pointing out that this complete obedience to the Chair of Peter began with Francis, Pope Pius XI showed how it must be continued in his followers.

The Seraphic Father demands that the rule and life of the Lesser Brothers should be 'to observe the holy Gospel of our Lord Jesus Christ, living in obedience, without property and in chastity,' not as he would interpret it or wish it to be, but rather, according to the pleasure of the Roman Pontiffs canonically elected.[11]

To think and feel with the Church in this way is to be one with the Church in mind, in spirit, in action. It does not mean that as Franciscans we can be eager only to cooperate, *co-operare*. Rather we have to feel with the Church, *sentire*. "Awareness of the mystery of the Church," Pope Paul VI wrote in *Ecclesiam Suam,* "results from a mature and living faith. From such a faith results that 'feeling with the Church,' which fills the Christian who has been raised in the school of the Gospel."[12] Pointing up this ideal, the same Pope said to an audience of sisters, which included a group of Poor Clares:

Feeling with the Church is felt less and less cultivated in certain religious families because they live apart and find within the framework of their own community all the objects of their immediate interest. They know little of what happens outside the framework of their occupations, to which they are completely dedicated. At times it happens their religious life thus has

limited horizons — not only regarding the development of the things of this world, but also regarding
the life of the Church, its events, its thoughts, its
teachings, its spiritual fervor, its sorrows, and its
fortunes. This is not an ideal attitude. . . .[13]

Like Francis, we should adapt to the milieu in which
the Church and order find themselves today. This is why
the words of the popes to us should be paternal guides interpreting our life for us. Their words express the will of
our God and Savior for us.

Throughout the years, the popes have written innumerable addresses to the Franciscans, including three encyclicals, besides all the other encyclicals and addresses given
to the world in general. From these words we determine
how best we can live as loyal sons and daughters in the
Church.[14]

What Pius XII said to the Society of Jesus applies equally to us: there should be no place among us for the spirit
of "liberal questioning" which is characteristic of an un-
orthodox, uncatholic mentality, whereby one continually
questions the pronouncements coming from the Bishop of
Rome.[15]

However this does not mean that we should not attempt
to understand the meaning of the popes' words. One must
take into account several aspects before we can arrive at
this understanding. For instance, one must consider the
needs and trends of the times in which the popes speak.
Those to whom they speak must also be considered. Above
all, however, they must be understood as expressions of
the mind of the Chief Shepherd of the Spirit-guided
Church. This means, then, that they should be considered
in the context in which they were spoken.

We must keep in mind also that what the popes have said specifically to the Franciscans they have also, in their own way, said to other institutes. Because of this, some regard such words as having little value in determining our spirit in the Church. Yet, Karl Rahner has pointed out that the popes' habit of speaking "in vast and splendid terms about one thing, as though it were the one and only thing that mattered, and then on some other occasion lauding some other thing again, as though the whole of salvation depended on it,"[16] can be justified because of the very fact that we *are* Christians. "The Christian, because he accepts God as always One who is greater than all else, has never been a person for having just one idea, one method, one absolute way."[17]

With Rahner we can apply what the popes say regarding spirituality in general to what they say about the Franciscan mission in the Church:

> Take Pope Pius XII: he praises Mary as though to-day everything depended upon her; he writes an encyclical about the Sacred Heart as though it were the most important thing of all; no doubt he praised both religious congregations and third orders as though there were nothing in the world dearer to his heart than each of them in turn. We do not have to have any special liking for these alternations, as far as we ourselves are concerned. But they do embody the impartiality of a Christian man, who can lovingly enfold many things in his embrace without seriously thinking that any one of them is, in all literalness, the one and only absolute of religious life.[18]

We have promised to live our life in the Church, mirroring it in our lives as Franciscans. In our particular case, what the Church says to us as Franciscans through her visible heads, does have *particular* importance for us. Thus their words to us can never be taken lightly.

Affirming this stand, the constitutions of the Conventuals, in commenting on the text from the rule wherein St. Francis "promises obedience and reverence to the lord Pope Honorius and his successors canonically entering office,"[19] say:

> Because of the special promise which our Seraphic Father made to the Supreme Pontiff and to the Apostolic See, all the friars are subject to the Roman Pontiff as their highest superior. In the promise he made, all Friars Minor were included. All are bound to obey the pope not only as a Christian duty and by the command of Christ Jesus, but also because of their religious vow of obedience. As Christians, therefore, the friars are subject to all pontifical ordinances, unless explicitly exempted, and as Friars Minor they are under an especial obligation reverently to obey the Apostolic See and its Sacred Congregations in all decrees pertaining in any way to the declarations, modification, or reformation of the rule.[20]

Well might we add that we ought to "reverently obey" not only what refers directly to the rule of the order, but to our total life in the Church as well.

Plainly, if we are to be another St. Francis for the world in which we live, we cannot be content merely to look to his life alone. We must look to his spirit. This leads us to the popes, our "supreme directors,"[21] as Francis was led to the popes, that they might interpret our role and mission in the Church. In his letter to the ministers general, *Cum Natalicia,* in which Pope John makes it clear that

our vocation consists in making Francis live again by our
deeds, he concludes:

> In order to happily fulfill the desire of our heart —
> and indeed, to fulfill more perfectly the will of God
> Himself, you must always remain sons dedicated en-
> tirely to the Apostolic See as your rule and way of
> life demands as an example to all. . .[22]

Franciscan Life Sustained in the Liturgy
of the Church

Our role and mission in the Church will be sterile if
it springs from anything but the life and spirit of the
Church, for there can be no true life in a member or organ
of the Church not permeated with the life and spirit of
the whole Body. If our actions are going to continue the
salvific acts of Christ in time, then our hearts must beat
with the grace-giving pulse of his own Heart in the Mystical Body, the Church of God's people. "It is not a privilege," Pope Paul said,

> to remain on the fringe of the life of the Church and
> to build for oneself a spirituality which prescinds from
> the spread of the Word, of grace, and of love in the
> catholic community of the brothers of Christ.[23]

We ought to bear witness to the virtues Christ presented
to Francis in the Gospel which have always been the glory
and heritage of the order. Yet we also should remember
that these cannot be practiced outside a life of union with
Christ which flows from the sacramental life of the Church.
In Francis' eyes, this is a matter of our salvation: "Let us
all be firmly convinced that no one can be saved except
through the Blood of our Lord Jesus Christ and the holy
words of our Lord."[24] Not only is the liturgy a matter of

our salvation, it is a matter of the salvation of all the souls
we meet, for as Francis told us: "In any preaching you do,
admonish the people concerning repentance, and that nobody can be saved except he who receives the most holy
Body and Blood of our Lord."[25]

The liturgy of the Church, which means the continuation
of the salvific acts of Christ in our own day coupled with
our response, is the Church's *official* school of perfection
and holiness. Thus it is the most effective means of living
the Christ-life. "It should be clear to all then," Pope Pius
XII wrote in *Mediator Dei*, "that the worship rendered to
God by the Church in union with her divine head is the
most efficacious means of achieving sanctity."[26]

Not only is the liturgy the dynamic means of living the
life of Christ, or rather, the means by which Christ continues to live in us; it is in the liturgy that Christ, through
his Church, instructs us twentieth century apostles by
means of his holy Word. Pope John once said:

> On the sacred and blessed altar we see two particular-
> ly precious and venerable objects, a Book and a Chal-
> ice. . . . This is the task that is called to mind by the
> Book laid open upon the altar: to teach true doctrine,
> proper discipline of life, and the ways in which man
> can rise toward God. . . . Alongside the Book stands
> the Chalice. The most sacred and mysterious part of
> the Eucharistic liturgy centers around the Chalice of
> Jesus. . . . 'There is no perfection in Christian life or
> practice aside from participation in the Eucharistic
> banquet.'[27]

In order to reach the perfection for which we have been
made, the people of God need to hear his holy Word. In
the liturgy, God speaks to us about the conditions of the

New Covenant that we might show our willingness to ratify it by sharing in his Body and Blood.

If anyone realized this, it was Francis. At the Divine Liturgy, the Sacrifice of the New Covenant, Christ inspired Francis to found his order through the reading of his Word. In the liturgy Francis sealed his part of the Covenant with God to spread his kingdom throughout the world. In fact, the whole life of our Seraphic Father seems to be a visual expression of what Pope Paul VI said while he was Archbishop of Milan: "The liturgy is not only a means of *teaching* dogmatic truth; it is also a school of *holiness* and one of the principal means of uniting our souls with Christ."[28]

The noted Franciscan author, Cajetan Esser, shows why such a liturgically-orientated life is basic to the Franciscan ideal:

> There is no true Franciscan life apart from the Church . . . for the Franciscan who lives in complete union with the Church and through her and for her, and is not guided by personal likes and dislikes, will be led by such humble and believing obedience to the very heart of the mystery of the Church. His very Franciscanism will derive its vitality from the power which the living Church gives him, especially through the word of God and the sacraments. Thus will the fullness of the Franciscan life, lived in the Church and patterned after her life, be a source of grace and blessing, of healing and sanctification, for all members of the Church.[29]

There are Franciscans who are beginning to believe that the reason why the order may not have been as fruitful in the apostolate of reform as we might desire is precisely

because its members have not sufficiently nourished themselves from the life-giving sap of the spirituality of the
Church. Instead, they have falsely stressed the acquiring
of virtues as the *raison d'être* of the Franciscan interior
life. Meanwhile, even though they have been in good
faith, these Franciscans seem to have forgotten that such
a life can only be a life of virtuous *expression of Christ,*
living, loving, and acting through them.

CONCLUSION

By stressing these life-giving fountains of grace in the
liturgy of the Word and the liturgy of the sacraments, Franciscanism will again have the strength to be the vital force
in the *aggiornamento* of the Church which the popes expect. This is the only way it can be accomplished. Fr. James
O'Mahoney says, speaking of St. Francis: "If he inaugurated a new springtime in the history of Christian spirituality, it was just because the pulse of his own spiritual
life beat in harmony with the great pulse of Catholic
life."[30] If we, as twentieth-century followers of Francis, are
to inaugurate a second springtime of reform in the history
of Christian spirituality as the popes desire, so must the
same spirit and life of the Church be ours.

Chapter Two

THE LIFE OF PENANCE IN THE CHURCH

Some people believe Pope John was the "new St. Francis" the world anticipated to help renew it. Paradoxically, the last one to believe this would have been Pope John. He never would have thought *he* could do such a thing. Yet he did think such a reform could be accomplished by other followers of St. Francis. In fact, he showed his conviction soon after his election. On April 4, 1959, he sent a letter to the ministers general of the Franciscan obediences in which he wrote:

> On account of the amazing technical progress which is being made in the modern world, it is easy for men, thinking themselves sufficient unto themselves, to fall into atheism, or to fail to observe the law of God. Thus deprived of the spiritual sun, they are in danger of falling into an icy winter of soul. Now it is of the greatest importance in order that some hope of a brighter future might lessen this great and ever-threatening danger, that St. Francis, through the ministry and good works of his followers, return once again to this earth. Oh, if only he would come back to this world, where his memory is still so cherished, and

37

raise his voice to recall sinners to penance and charity:
to persuade them to turn their minds to higher and
better things.[1]

With these words, Pope John summarized the fundamental reason why he and all the modern popes look to the
sons and daughters of St. Francis to be the instruments of
personal, social, and church reform: "Oh, if only he would
come back to this world . . . and raise his voice to recall
sinners to *penance and charity:* to persuade them to turn
their minds to higher and better things."

The popes look to the children of Francis in the three
orders and the secular institutes to imitate their Father
in reforming society through penance and love. They base
this reform, as Francis based his, on the return to the Gospel of penance and love, on the imitation of Christ. Francis
always was and his children must always be the instruments of Christ, for it can only be upon Christ, who truly
reformed the world through his Gospel of penance spring-
ing from love, that any new reform will be able to be based.
As Leo XIII noted in his encyclical on St. Francis:

> Jesus Christ, the Savior of mankind, is the ever-new
> and perennial fountainhead of all the blessings which
> are showered upon us from the infinite goodness of
> God; so that, just as he once saved the world, so he
> carries out salvation through all ages. . . . Whenever,
> therefore, as a result either of human weakness or mal-
> ice, mankind lapses into corruption and needs special
> assistance to free itself, it must resort to Jesus Christ
> as its chief and safest recourse. Such is his divine
> power and so great is its efficacy, that in it are found
> the defense against all dangers and the remedy for all
> ailments. Such a cure is certain if only the world be

brought back to the profession of Christian truth and
to the evangelical precepts of life.[2]

It was Christ, who, to use the words of Pope John referring to Francis, *first* raised "his voice to recall sinners
to penance and charity: to persuade them to turn their
minds to higher and better things." In fact, his Gospel is
a summary, a culmination, of the basic message of salvation history. It is a call to personal penance which
springs from love, in order that the peace of social reform
might be effected. To effect this reform in the hearts of
men is the reason for the existence of the Franciscan
order.

PENANCE IN SALVATION HISTORY

All of salvation history can be summed up in the concept
of a dialogue of love. In the words of Pope Paul VI:

> We need to keep ever present this ineffable, yet real
> relationship of the dialogue, which God the Father,
> through Christ in the Spirit, has offered to us and
> established with us, if we are to understand the re-
> lationship which we — the Church — must strive to
> establish and foster with the human race. The dialogue
> of salvation was opened spontaneously on the initi-
> ative of God: 'he first loved us' (1 Jn. 4, 10).[3]

God has loved us with an everlasting love in Christ. He
has given us Christ to be our model and draw us to himself
so that, in him, we might make a return of love to God.
Christ has shown us that the life of penance is the return
of love. In fact, penance properly conceived *is* love. It
is a *metanoia* — basically a re-orientation or conversion of
one's whole self from the "I" of the individual to the "you"

of God. In this encounter of the "I" and the "you," and
in the mutual exchange of life and love which results in
the "we," the grace of God invades our hearts, flooding
us with his peace. Here, then, is the *metanoia* toward
God in Christ, "Christ is our living peace."[4] With Christ,
the Prince of Peace, living and reigning in our hearts, God
continues his kingdom in time.

In order to understand the role of Franciscanism in
effecting this reform which the popes desire in individuals
and society in general, it is extremely necessary to understand the true meaning of penance. Penance, for the
prophets, for Christ, and for Francis, was not the accumu-
lation of various fastings, mortifications, or disciplines, although they definitely were part of it. Penance, conceived
as *metanoia*, means something more basic, something more
necessary — and more beautiful. It is simply conversion.
"Yet even now, says the Lord, return to me with your whole
heart, with fasting, and weeping, and mourning; rend your
hearts, not your garments, and return to the Lord, your
God."[5]

All of salvation history tells the story of penance or the
lack of it. As Pope John wrote in *Poenitentiam Agere:*

> We only have to open the sacred books of the Old
> and New Testament to realize one thing: it was never
> God's will to reveal himself in any solemn encounter
> with mortal men — to speak in human terms — with-
> out first calling them to prayer and penance.[6]

Penance is the conversion of one's heart and mind, a
change from one's stress on the "I" to the "you." It implies going out to something better — to the "you," leaving
something not so good behind — the "I." This expresses
the true scriptural meaning of penance. St. Lawrence of

Brindisi, the Capuchin Doctor, writes, "Penance in the divine writings is called a conversion,"[7] and in another place, "In Greek, penance is called a *metanoia* and *metanoia* means repentance, a return, a change of outlook, a change and reversal of the sentiments of the heart."[8]

With this concept of penance as a foundation, Nevin Crosby O.F.M.Cap., writes:

> In the language of scripture, penance is not a virtue; it is a way of life. It is man's wholehearted response to God's appeals of love. Man, through God's grace, begins to understand the love of God which has been showered upon him. Understanding that love, he is moved to respond by a similar love. That love, he discovers, must take the form of a conversion, a turning aside from his former sinful life and a turning toward the God who loves him.[9]

Penance in the Old Testament

In the Old Testament we read that the cries for this change of heart, for the most part, fell on deaf ears. "The dialogue of salvation," Pope Paul VI wrote in *Ecclesiam Suam,*

> did not physically force anyone to accept it; it was a tremendous appeal of love which, although placing a vast responsibility on those toward whom it was directed (cf. Mt. 11, 21), nevertheless left them free to respond to it or to reject it.[10]

The Old Testament tells the sad story of the few who responded to the pleas of God through his prophets. These, the prophets began to realize, would be the only ones who would enter the kingdom. These would be the faithful "remnant" of God's people who would recognize God's love and thus turn to him with their whole hearts. These would be the "little ones," the *anawim*, and to them would it be given to know the meaning of the kingdom of God. As the Holy Spirit said through the prophet Micah:

> I will gather you, O Jacob, each and every one, I will assemble all the remnant of Israel; I will group them like a flock in the fold. . . . With a leader to break the path they shall burst open the gate and go out through it; their king shall go before them, and the Lord at their head. . . . On that day, says the Lord, I will gather the lame, and I will assemble the out-casts, and those whom I have afflicted. I will make of the lame a remnant, and of those driven far off a strong nation; and the Lord shall be king over them on Mount Sion, from now on forever.[11]

Why, when it was ordained by God's salvific will that the message of the prophets should be preached to all God's people, did the message go unheeded? Because only a few would commit themselves to a response. This was the remnant. It would be "like a flock in the fold." It would be to this flock that a Shepherd, a Lord, would come. The flock need not fear; to them would be given the kingdom. Not only would this kingdom be one of the future inheritance, it would also exist as an earthly kingdom wherein his reign would be effectual in the submission of men's hearts to his law of love. Centuries before the fulfillment of God's promise, Jeremiah indicated such an advent would fulfill the covenant in the truest sense of the word.

> The days are coming, says the Lord, when I will make a new covenant with the house of Israel and the house of Juda. It will not be like the covenant I

made with their fathers the day I took them by the hand to lead them forth from the land of Egypt; for they broke my covenant, and I had to show myself their master, says the Lord. But this is the covenant which I will make with the house of Israel after those days, says the Lord. I will place my law within them, and write it upon their hearts, I will be their God and they shall be my people. No longer will they have to teach their friends and kinsmen how to know the Lord. All, from the last to the greatest, shall know me, says the Lord, for I will forgive their evildoing and remember their sin no more.[12]

Penance in the New Testament

After hundreds of years of waiting for their Messiah, finally, "in the fulness of time," God sent John the Baptist to be the precursor of the New Covenant. "In due course, John the Baptist arrived, preaching in the Judean desert: 'You must change your hearts — for the kingdom of heaven has arrived?' "[13] John, just as the prophets before him, had but one message, one gospel: penance, the conversion of hearts to God. This alone would prepare the way for the Lord and make way for his kingdom. This alone would result in the reign of Christ in the hearts of men.

In his encyclical on penance, Pope John pointed out how Christ continued to stress the necessity of personal conversion in all his encounters with men.

These calls to penance did not stop when the Son of God became incarnate. On the contrary, they even became more insistent. At the very beginning of his preaching, John the Baptist had proclaimed: 'You must change your hearts — for the kingdom of heaven has arrived!' (Mt. 3, 2). Jesus inaugurated his saving

mission in the same manner. He did not begin by re-
vealing the principal truths of the faith. He insisted
first that the soul must repent of every trace of sin that
could render it impervious to the message of eternal
salvation: "From that time Jesus began to preach and
to say, 'You must change your hearts — for the kingdom of Heaven has arrived!' (Mt. 4, 17).[14]

If we go to the other gospels, we discover the same
underlying theme St. Matthew shows in his gospel, namely, the attitudes needed for incorporation into the kingdom. For instance, St. Mark summarizes the hundreds of
years of preparation that preceded the Lord with the
first words Christ spoke in his inaugural appearance in
Galilee.

> It was after John's arrest that Jesus came into Galilee,
> proclaiming the gospel of God, saying: 'The time
> has come at last — the kingdom of God has arrived.
> You must change your hearts and minds and believe
> in the good news.'[15]

Yet once again, as of old, only the *anawim* would respond with a determined decision for him. Because he
realized this, Christ concentrated on proclaiming the kingdom to them. In fact, in the passage of St. Luke where
Christ first indicates he fulfills the Old Testament Covenant, we read:

> Then he came to Nazareth where he had been
> brought up and, according to his custom, went to the
> synagogue on the Sabbath day. He stood up to read
> the scripture and the book of the prophet Isaiah was
> handed to him. He opened the book and found the
> place where these words are written —

" 'The Spirit of the Lord is upon me,
Because he anointed me
    to preach good tidings to the poor:
He hath sent me
    To proclaim release to the captives,
    And recovering of sight to the blind,
    To set at liberty them that are bruised,
    To proclaim the acceptable year of the Lord.'

Then he shut the book, handed it back to the attendant and resumed his seat. Every eye in the synagogue was fixed upon him and he began to tell them,

" 'This day this scripture has been fulfilled, while you have been listening to it!'[16]

Christ knew so well that only the poor, the little ones, would be given the kingdom. We have his own word for this.

It was at this time that the disciples came to Jesus with the question, 'Who is really greatest in the kingdom of heaven?' Jesus called a little child to his side and set him on his feet in the middle of them all. 'Believe me,' he said, 'unless you change your whole outlook and become like little children you will never enter the kingdom of heaven. It is the man who can be as humble as this little child who is the greatest in the kingdom of heaven.'[17]

In order that Christ might establish his kingdom or reign within their hearts, they had to change their whole outlook from the "I" to the "you" by abiding by the law of the New Covenant, the law of love. By inflaming the hearts of the people of God, as he did the disciples on the way

to Emmaus, he sought to convert them, to turn them to
God.

Christ's whole life in the gospels is a story of one witnessing to the love of God for men. It was in this personal
dialogue that men came to truly understand the love of
God for them, namely, that he had given them his own
Son. As Pope John noted, in fact, "He was even more vehe-
ment than the prophets in his demands that those who
listened to him must undergo a complete change of heart
and submit in perfect sincerity to all the laws of the Supreme God. 'For behold,' he had said, 'the Kingdom of God
is within you' (Lk. 17, 21)."[18] Yet, sad to say, Christ's whole
life tells the story of the same lack of response to the message which was preached by the prophets.

God promised his people someone to lead them in their
return to himself: "I will give them a heart with which to
understand that I am the Lord," he had said to Jeremiah;
"they shall be my people and I will be their God, for they
shall return to me with their whole heart."[19] "I will give
them a heart with which to understand that I am the Lord,"
God said. So he gave them his Sacred Heart that they
might learn about him. That Sacred Heart had, in turn,
said to man, "Put on my yoke and learn from me. For I
am gentle and humble in heart."[20] His yoke was the yoke of
a child's, the yoke of a true son always ready to fulfill
the will of his father. In fact Christ's whole life was one
of service, not only to his Father, but to all men. He stood
in our midst as one who serves, saying of himself, ". . . the
Son of Man himself has not come to be served but to serve,
and to give his life to set many others free."[21] He was the
true Servant of God, "giving us an example," that as he
served, so should we.

At the height of his obedience and service, he was lifted

up. The heart that truly understood the love of God was pierced that all men might enter and be transformed into him that they might return to God in the Spirit of his Love. Christ died in the greatest act of loving service the world has known. He founded the Church which sprang from that open side and pierced heart that he might incorporate all the people of God into the heavenly kingdom. He did this that his Church, his kingdom, might be like him — standing in the world as one who serves. But again, only the few little ones would listen.

Penance in the Life of Francis

As the centuries after his ascension wore on, the message Christ proclaimed as well as his example grew dimmer and dimmer. In the light and luxury of the years that followed, the Gospel of God gave way to the gospel of man. Yet, despite the fact that so many of his people turned away from him, God in his mercy turned his heart to them and knew he would send another patriarch, another prophet, to his people. "In the fulness of time," after twelve centuries, he looked upon the world with mercy and love and raised up another instrument, the Patriarch of Assisi, the Poverello of Umbria. Pope Leo XIII summed up succinctly what has been said when he wrote:

Now whenever conditions such as we have indicated come about, at the same time the providential moment for applying the remedy arrives. God always seems opportunely to raise up on earth a man who is not just one of the many, but singular and raised above the rest and charges him with the task of restoring healthy social conditions. This is precisely what came to pass toward the end of the twelfth century and somewhat later; the instrument chosen to accomplish this great task was Francis.[22]

More recently, Pope Pius XII said much the same when he addressed the Franciscans soon after his election in 1939:

> But when the human race was thus rushing to the abyss, God mercifully came to its help and steadied it through the work of Sts. Francis and Dominic and their consecrated armies. Thereupon, with reverence for the Roman Church aroused by means of the spirit of penance, the merit of poverty, and the loveliness of the Gospel held in the highest esteem, the manners and customs of the nations suddenly shone forth with a marvelous splendor of faith and civilization.[23]

Interestingly, the first thing Pius XII mentions as the fruit of the work of Dominic and Francis is that "reverence for the Roman Church" was "aroused by means of the spirit of penance." If there ever was one who recalled "sinners to penance and charity: to persuade them to turn their minds to higher and better things,"[24] and live according to the Gospel through the spirit and life of the Church in penance, it was Francis. His whole spirituality was this kind of a response to the love of God.

God loved Francis with an infinite love and in Christ crucified, he had drawn him to himself. With Francis, as with the world itself, the dialogue of salvation began with the divine goodness.[25] God's overwhelming goodness swept Francis out of himself, out of his "I," and into God's arms. In his "Page of Praises for Brother Leo," our Seraphic Father expresses the whole foundation for his spirit of penance with a canticle of God's loving goodness showing how he truly understood that God is love for us. For Francis it did not matter that much that we love God, although he couldn't help but make a return of love to God. What was the important thing, though, was that God, in his merciful goodness, had first loved *us:* For this reason he wrote,

> You alone are holy, O Lord God,
>> you are he who performs things wondrous.
> You are strong. You are full of majesty.
> You are most high. You are the King Almighty —
>> you, holy Father, King of Heaven and Earth.
> You are the Lord God,
>> threefold and one and all that is good.
>
> You are what is good, all that is good,
>> the Sovereign Good, the Lord God true and loving.
> You are charity and love. You are wisdom.
> You are humility. You are patience. You are
>> assurance. You are restfulness.
> You are joy and gladness.
>> You are justice and temperance.
>
> You are the wealth desirable.
>> You are beauty. You are gentleness.
> You protect. You guard and defend.
> You are our hope. You are our faith.
>> You are our relish.
> You are our eternal life, great and wondrous Lord,
>> God almighty, Savior merciful.[26]

The loving goodness of God was the driving force in Francis' whole reform, both personal and social. In fact, we can say this characterizes Francis' spirituality. In the words of Pope Pius XII,

There is a Franciscan doctrine in accordance with
which God is holy, is great, but above all is good, indeed the Supreme Good. For in this doctrine God is
love: he lives by love, creates by love, becomes flesh
and redeems and now sanctifies, for love.[27]

In this realization of the loving goodness God has
shown us, Francis burned with an intense desire to return that love. Love, he knew, can be repaid only by love.
God's turning to man can be repaid only by man's turning
to God. God alone could be his sufficiency; Christ and his
Spirit alone could be his content.

This great desire of Francis drove him on to reproduce
in himself the likeness of God's Son that this conversion
might be complete. Thus Francis embraced the gospels
with their message of penance-love. Here he discovered
God's Love Incarnate, showing men how to make such a
return. Christ, the Goodness of God Incarnate, became the
subject of Francis' every thought, meditation, and imitation — so much so that Pius XII could also say,

There is a Franciscan way of contemplating Jesus: the
meeting of uncreated Love with created love. Simi-
larly, there is a method of loving Jesus and of imitating him: in reality it sees the Man-God, and prefers to
consider him in his holy humanity, because it reveals
him more clearly and, as it were, allows him to be
touched. From this arises a burning devotion to the
Incarnation and the Passion of Jesus, because these
mysteries allow us to see God, not so much in his
glory, nor in his omnipotent grandeur, nor in his eternal triumph, as rather in his human love — so tender
in the manger, so sorrowful on the cross.[28]

In return for this loving goodness he found revealed in every page of the gospels, Francis could only try to give himself completely to Christ as an instrument that Christ might once again reform the world through him. "Was it not this whole-hearted following of the Christ of the Crib, the Christ of the Cross, and the Christ of the Tabernacle that transformed the life and being of the Little Poor Man?" Pope Paul VI has asked. "Was it not this total surrender to the Christ of the Gospel that fashioned the very depths of the soul of Francis?"[29]

Because God had given his Heart to man, Francis' whole ideal was to return man's heart to God. This is why for Francis penance was truly love itself. The love and enthusiasm Francis showed to the world in his return of heart to God is so evident in the following passage which he wrote, that it deserves to be quoted at length:

> With all our heart and soul and mind and strength and fortitude and understanding and all our faculties; with all our endeavor, affection, and yearning; with all we desire and will, let us all love God the Lord, who has given and still gives us all our whole body, soul, and life; who has created and redeemed us and only in his mercy will save us; who has done and keeps doing everything good to us, miserable and wretched, corrupt and foul, ungrateful and wicked as we are.

> So let us desire nothing else, wish for nothing else, take pleasure and delight in nothing else but our Creator, Redeemer, and Savior, the only true God, who is the perfect good, everything good; wholly good, the true and sovereign good; he who alone is good, loving and gentle, sweet and lovable; he who alone is holy,

just, true, and fair; who alone is kind, innocent, and
clean; from whom, and through whom, and in whom
is all pardon, all grace, and all glory for all the re-
pentant and the just and for all the blessed rejoicing
together in heaven.

Then let nothing hinder us, nothing keep us apart,
nothing get in the way. All over, everywhere, at every
hour and at any time, day after day and without ceas-
ing let us all believe in him with a true and humble
faith, cherish him in our heart, and love, honor, adore,
serve, praise, and bless him, glorify, exalt, and extol
him, and give thanks to him, the most high, sovereign,
eternal God, in Trinity and Unity, Father, Son, and
Holy Spirit, the Creator of all things, the Savior of
all who have faith and hope and love for him; who is
without beginning and without end, unchangeable,
invisible, unutterable, ineffable, incomprehensible,
unfathomable, blest, worthy of praise, glorious, exalted above all, sublime, supreme, yet sweet, lovable,
delightful, and always altogether desirable beyond
everything forever and ever.[30]

Truly this is the life of penance. This is the conversion
of one's heart to God. This is the Franciscan way of loving
God and living God.

We have already equated penance with love. Since love
is the foundation of perfection, so too is penance. This is
probably why Pope John wrote, "No individual Christian
can grow in perfection, nor can Christianity itself gain in
vigor, except that it be on this basis of penance."[31]

Such a penance, such a love, is turning one's heart to
God to do his will. It is serving the will of others, as our
Redeemer and Savior showed us.

Penance in the Apostolate of Francis

Francis realized perfectly that not just he nor his sons and daughters, but all men were created to be members of the kingdom of God. Thus he realized all men are called to the life of penance. He referred to himself as the Herald of the Great King because it was his aim to preach penance to the whole world, to announce the Good News of the kingdom to all men. The reform demanded by Christ was that preached by Francis: turn to God in penance and love and you will find peace. Love your neighbor, learn to serve him, and the world will find peace. This formed the basis of his reform — turn to God yourself and you will draw others with you. Individual reform became the basis for social reform.

Francis knew the dialogue of salvation was made accessible to all. He knew it was destined for all without exception.[32] Because he knew this he preached to all men.

Francis also knew that, just as in the days of the prophets, only a remnant would listen and thus become fit to be members of the kingdom. He knew they could be incorporated in the kingdom only if they served its laws, especially the law of love. The Poverello must have thought about this very often, and because of this he must have been led to that passage in the Gospel which makes it clear that since God is the ruler in the kingdom, only those who convert and turn to him and do his will will be its members. One day, the gospels tell us, Christ was preaching near Jerusalem.

> Then his mother and his brothers arrived. They stood outside the house and sent a message asking him to come out to them. There was a crowd sitting round when the message was brought telling him, 'Your

mother and your brothers are outside looking for you.'
Jesus replied, 'And who are really my mother and my
brothers?' And he looked round at the faces of those
sitting in a circle about him. 'Look!' he said, 'my
mother and brothers are here. Anyone who does the
will of God is brother and sister and mother to
me.'[33]

The words of the Herald of the Great King in his "Letter
to all the Faithful" seem like a living commentary on this
passage:

And all who act thus and persevere to the end — the
Spirit of the Lord shall rest on them and make his
home and abode in them, and they shall be children
of the heavenly Father, whose work they do, and they
are the spouses, brothers, and mothers of our Lord Jesus Christ. We are his spouses when through the Holy
Spirit the faithful soul is united with Jesus Christ. We
are his brothers when we do the will of his Father, who
is in heaven. We are his mothers when we carry him
about in our heart and person by means of love and
clean and sincere conscience, and we give birth to
him by means of our holy actions, which should shine
as an example to others.[34]

Is not precisely this the Franciscan message we must
announce to the world? Entrance into the kingdom of
God rests in turning to God by doing his will, in love. By
serving God's will, by giving birth to him in our actions,
we will bear witness to Christ to others, and, in so doing,
lead them to convert in their hearts, to embrace the life of
penance as well. This is a basic point in the life of penance: the drawing of *others* to turn to God. This is the

new *Weltanschauung*, the true world outlook, which we find in the gospels.

Penance is a personal matter, it is true; but if it is truly lived, is it not also something which can have a marked influence on the world? Cajetan Esser and Englebert Grau insist, in speaking of its influence on the Church:

> The goal of the life of penance is not primarily the personal sanctification of the individual Christian, but the upbuilding of the Church of Christ. Who undertakes such a life with the blessing of the Church and seeks to perfect it in the Church serves thereby to build up her inner life. This indeed Innocent III had predicted of St. Francis: 'Truly, this is that man who by his work and doctrine will support the Church of Christ.'[35]

This same spirit can influence society in general. First of all, because of the unity of the human race, there is no good action of man which does not have reverberations on the whole of society. Secondly, the spirit of penance, which is the expression of love, brings to the hearts of men that peace which the world cannot give. Because the world and all the souls in the world so ache for this peace, they will be drawn to imitate the man who possesses it.

Here, then, we find the reason why the popes have insisted on the value of the Franciscan reform movement as a major instrument in our age of reform. The popes have not asked for a return to the ideal of Francis, thinking of it as something which might give us a good feeling, for sentiment's sake. They ask for the return of Francis because of what Francis can *do*. If his spirit would truly be understood, if the members of his three orders and the secular institutes would understand that by their vocation in the Church they are committed, *obligated*, to reform the world and bring it back to true Gospel principles, the real St. Francis would live again.

PENANCE IN THE DIALOGUE

In 1932, Pope Pius XI wrote in *Caritate Christi Compulsi*,

> Prayer and penance are the two potent inspirations sent to us at this time by God, that we may bring back to him our wayward human race that wanders aimlessly without a guide. They are the inspirations that will disperse and remedy the first and foremost cause of all rebellion and unrest, man's revolt against God.[36]

As children of St. Francis, we have a guide to offer our wayward human race — the universal appeal of our Seraphic Father. We have a remedy for man's revolt against God — the powerful message of God's loving goodness towards us to which we can respond with a return of love, with a change of heart.

This must always be the central theme in our life. Franciscanism means Christ. Christ means the world for God. Life cannot be just the "I" of ourselves, or even the "you" of Christ, but, in Christ, the center of the world, it must be the "we" of all men. Our hearts must be as big as the world; they must embrace it because Christ lives, loves, and acts through us and this is the way he wants it to be. "Go therefore," he tells us.

We cannot have the spirit of Christ within us and not give it to the world. We cannot burn with the love of God within us without the flame shooting through our every thought, word, and action. The world must see in

us other Christs as it once saw Christ in Francis. Only then
will the world become truly Christian. This is why the
popes insist we can never divorce our life from the apostolate, which is the expression of Christ in the world. This is
our role in continuing the dialogue of salvation. "The duty
consonant with the patrimony received from Christ," Pope
Paul has written,

> is that of spreading, offering, and announcing it to
> others. Well do we know that 'You, then, are to go
> and make disciples of all nations' (Mt. 28, 19) is the
> last command of Christ to his Apostles. By the very
> term 'apostles' these men define their inescapable mis-
> sion. To this internal drive of charity which tends to
> become the external gift of charity we can give the
> name of dialogue. . . [37]

This is our heritage; the heritage of salvation history continued in us.

We may lack material goods or talents, but with our
hearts turned toward God, we have his Spirit to pour
out upon the earth. This is our apostolate; we should look
for nothing more. Like Pope Paul, we should not fear it;
we should embrace it. Cardinal Suenens has given us a very
fine definition of such an apostolate which flows from one's
love of God expressing itself in love for all men: "Suffice
it to say," he writes,

> that the apostolate is the extension of Christ's mission
> in and through the Church, a mission which consists
> of giving God to the world, of acting in such a man-
> ner that men come to know God, to love him and
> serve him, to take their nourishment from him, and
> to live the whole of the Gospel in every aspect of
> their whole lives.[38]

Clearly, as we have seen,[39] such an exterior life flows only from an interior life animated by the spirit and life of the Church. If our hearts are on fire for the world, the flame of our love cannot help but spread over the earth — or at the very least, over that part of the earth with which we come in contact. Whatever we encounter should be made better because of Christ within us.

We Franciscans, who have "a method of loving Jesus and of imitating him,"[40] have a perfect way to win the world to Christ through the universal appeal of our Seraphic Father. He was a man set on fire with love. All the world loves such a lover.

The Witness of Francis

The world is instinctively drawn to the lover. We have seen this in the case of Pope John XXIII. This explains why the world, down through the centuries, has been drawn to Francis. Many times, though, in being drawn to Francis, the souls in the world have unconsciously drawn closer to Christ, the Heart of Love. As Pope Paul said on the feast of St. Francis, 1964, St. Francis has been venerated

> at every level of society and not only by Catholics and other Christians, but by the members of other religions as well. The reason for this is the force, attraction, and suggestion which St. Francis continues and will continue to exercise over men. Such a power results from the efforts by which the Saint sought faithfully to imitate Christ.[41]

Francis had converted to God to such an extent that Christ acted through him. Thus, for him, to live really was Christ. As Pope Pius XI wrote in *Rite Expiatis:*

While it is presumptuous to make comparisons be-

tween the heroes of sanctity who have been called
to their heavenly home and whom the Holy Spirit has
chosen here below, one for this task, another for that
— comparisons which, arising, as they generally do,
from inordinate motives, are altogether futile and
even at times offensive to God, the author of sanctity,
— nevertheless it would appear that in no one has
the image of Christ our Lord and the ideal of the
Gospel life been more faithfully and strikingly expressed than in Francis. This is why he called himself
'the Herald of the Great King.' This is also why he
has justly been called 'the Second Christ,' *alter Chris-
tus* — because he has appeared as Christ re-incarnated
to his contemporaries and to later ages, with the result that he lives today in the eyes of men and will
live unto all posterity.[42]

Today we need Francis. If we summarize all the
world's problems — its race problems, population problems, moral problems, we see they all basically stem from
selfishness of some sort or another. They stem from a lack
of genuine love.[43]

The one solution to all these problems is reform, penance
as Francis saw it, penance *as* love — the transfer of the
selfishness of the "I" to the otherness of the "you" and in
this otherness to find the "we" of humanity, the "we" which
speaks for every man. This is why if men can reform themselves, the world will be reformed. Pope Benedict XV
wrote about Francis:

Burning with a seraphic love of God and man, Francis could not contain his charity within his heart; he
had to pour it out upon everyone. Hence, though he
began by reforming the private and domestic life of

his followers and adorned them with Christian virtues, as though he might have seemed to want nothing
more, still he had no intention of contenting himself with that alone. He used the reformation of individuals as a means to arouse in the hearts of the
people a love of Christian wisdom and to win all
unto Jesus Christ.[44]

Penance and World Reform

Francis realized he was responsible for the world as part
of the universal "we." In order to turn its heart to God, he
had to be oriented completely around Christ, the center,
the Omega Point of the universe.

The ideal Francis had in his day remains the same in
ours. "By now," Pope John wrote in *La Nostra Prima,*

> every member of the Holy Roman Church is per-
> meated by this principle: that, insofar as he is a Catho-
> lic, he is, and considers himself to be, a citizen of the
> whole world, just as Christ is the adored Savior of the
> world, *Salvator Mundi.*[45]

We are citizens of the whole world. Like Francis, the
world is ours to give to Christ, to Christianize. We have
no better way to do this than through the example of Francis. The message of Francis echoes the message of Christ;
both announce the gospel of penance. Pope Paul has
noted that this Christian message is not a prophecy of con-
demnation. Rather it is, he says, a call to penance in order
to call to salvation.[46] Penance, then, just as love, is indispen-
sable for salvation. It consists in a personal feeling of responsibility for those we must love and this, for the follower of Francis, means responsibility for all men; in body,
soul, and spirit. This maps our way of salvation. It maps
the way we will save the world.

As Pope Paul has pointed out, we will convert the world by loving it and turning to it.

> We will love our brothers, whether they be close or distant. We will love our own fatherland, and we will love other fatherlands. We will love our friends, and we will love our enemies. We will love Catholics, and we will love schismatics, Protestants, Anglicans, the indifferent, Moslems, pagans, atheists.
>
> We will love all social classes, but particularly those which have the most need of help, of assistance, of betterment. We will love the very young and the very old, the poor, and the sick.
>
> We will love those who mock us, who despise us, who stand in our way, who persecute us. We will love those who are worthy of love, and those who are unworthy. We will love those who fight against us: we will love our times, our community, our technical skills, our art, our sport, our world.
>
> We will love and we will try to understand, to have compassion, to think well of others, to serve them, to bear with them. We will love with the heart of Christ. . . [47]

CONCLUSION

With Francis as our guide, we can bring this love, this salvation to the world. By penetrating a bit deeper into his life, by studying his specific virtues and the way he went about reforming men's lives we can show the world the peace that results in hearts which turn to God in love. Once again, we can bring about a rebirth of his message in the hearts and actions of men.

Part Two

RETURN TO THE IDEAL
OF FRANCIS

Chapter Three

THE FIRE WITHIN

Our lives as Christians and followers of the man who founded his order upon the Gospel must be based upon the Gospel. "The Gospel is light, it is newness, it is energy, it is rebirth, it is salvation," Pope Paul wrote in *Ecclesiam Suam:*

> Thus it both creates and defines a type of new life, about which the New Testament teaches a continuous and remarkable lesson such as is found in the warning of St. Paul: 'Don't let the world around you squeeze you into its own mold, but let God remold your minds from within, so that you may prove in practice that the plan of God for you is good, meets all his demands and moves toward the goal of true maturity'" (Rom. 12,2).[1]

We become mature in Christ by reflecting continually on his Gospel message. The good news preached by Christ demands a ready heart, an intense spirit of faith, and even a life of union with God in order to understand it, in order to truly *know* it in the Semitic sense of the word — to have intimate experience of the word. When we truly know something, we become alive with what we know.

If we truly know *the* Word, Christ, as depicted in the gospels, we become alive with Christ experientially.

Few men in history have been able to go directly to the gospels from the onset of their spiritual life without a guide other than the Spirit in the Church. In fact, the very first hearers of the Gospel message did not even understand the good news, and they had the advantage of the visual aid *par excellence*. From the descriptions they themselves have given us, we are sure that the apostles did not understand the events which we read about in the gospels until after the Resurrection, when they received the special grace of the Spirit. These events which they did not understand by their own powers of nature are the events we read about today. This is why no one can understand their true meaning without the Spirit-guided testimony of the Church. This is also why few can understand their meaning even with this.

It was both the genius and the special grace of St. Francis not to need a human guide, except in the guidance of the Church. With the aid of the Spirit-guided Church, it was his special grace to draw his spirituality directly from the Gospel.[2] ". . . there was nobody to show me what to do; but the Most High himself revealed to me that I was to live according to the form of the Holy Gospel."[3]

"The ideal of perfection which Francis proposes to all his children is not that of a minimized version of Christ, cut down to suit their wants and adapted to human rationalization or a restricted earthly view of things," Pope Paul said to the Franciscans,

> but it is rather the Christ of the Gospel, pictured to us by Francis in his own person. It is Christ, humble and meek, poor and obedient, reviled and humiliated;

it is the Christ of Bethlehem and Nazareth, the Christ
of the cross and the altar. It is the actual living Christ
whom he loved with passionate ardor and whom he
followed with enthusiasm; the Christ who operates
through every one of us in concrete, everyday life; the
Christ who is present among us in the person of the
poor and all the members of his Mystical Body, especially its suffering and sick members; the Christ who,
in all truth, is for souls 'the Way, the Truth, and the
Life.'[4]

IDENTIFYING WITH CHRIST

Christ said, "*I am the Way.*" Through his Spirit, he im-
planted in Francis the grace for him and his children to
better understand the meaning of his Way. St. Clare realized this. This is why she did not go directly to the Gospel
but rather went to the Gospel *through* her Father,
St. Francis. "The Son of God became for us the Way (Jn.
14, 16)," she wrote in her *Testament*, "and that Way our
Blessed Father Francis, his true lover and imitator, has
shown and taught us by word and example."[5]

We have become Franciscans in order to follow the Way
in the manner St. Francis has laid down in the rule, which
is the mirror of the gospels. For us, this is truly "the hope
of our salvation."[6] This is the best way to reform ourselves
as well as society, for in doing this we will be fulfilling the
will of God. In his encyclical on St. Francis, Pope Benedict XV made it clear that:

> When all is said and done, it is a question of open-
> ing to as many as possible the following of Francis
> on the path and the return to Christ, on which return
> rests Our greatest hope of common salvation. We may

justly apply the words of St. Paul: 'Copy me, my
brothers, as I copy Christ Himself' (1 Cor. 11, 1), to
Francis who, by copying Christ, has become his most
perfect image and likeness.[7]

"Copy me," Francis tells us. "Copy me as I copy Christ."
Francis copied Christ by living his life in union with the
life of the Church, the liturgy, the renewal of the salvific
acts of Christ recounted in the gospels. It is easy to see
then, that Francis expressed his union with Christ by
stressing in his life those virtues of Christ which are depicted in the Gospel. Francis laid special stress on those
virtues in which our Lord showed his greatest love for us.
This is why all the virtues, for Francis, can be reduced to
expressions of love.

The Virtues of Christ

There are no specific "Franciscan" virtues. There are
only *Christ*-ian virtues. What we call "Franciscan" virtues
merely express the life of Christ which his Spirit in the
Church inspired Francis to embrace in a special way. Thus
there can be no thought of the primacy of Francis' spirituality over that of the founders of other religious institutes. All followed the Whole Christ. With Christ as the
Head of the Church there can be but one spirituality, the
spirituality of the Church. There can be but accidental
manifestations of this one spirituality in the various institutes. In the words of Pius XII's *Mystici Corporis:*

> The whole Body of the Church as well as all the in-
> dividual members should bear resemblance to Christ.
> This is his will. We realize this when, following in the
> footsteps of her Founder, the Church teaches, governs,
> and offers the Divine Sacrifice. We see this realized

when she embraces the evangelical counsels, reflecting the Redeemer's poverty, obedience, and virginal purity. Enriched with institutes of many different kinds, as with so many precious jewels, she reflects Christ deep in prayer on the mountain, preaching to the people, healing the sick and wounded, and bringing back sinners to the path of virtue, or, in a word, going about doing good to all.[8]

An institute in the Church, like all the cells and members, has no meaning apart from Christ, the Head. The cell cannot stand by itself. It has no meaning outside the Body.[9]

Christian Virtues of Francis

We must participate in the life of the Mystical Body through *Its* life which is the liturgy. Though we have stressed the role of the liturgy in *forming* us in the life and mind of Christ, nevertheless we have to *express* this life and mind of Christ through our actions. This expression of the life and mind of Christ manifests itself in the imitation of his virtues as Francis has shown us.

We can say that since we have the life of Christ in us through the liturgy, it is really Christ himself who lives these virtues through us. As Francis said in his famous "Salute to the Virtues:" "All you most holy virtues, may the Lord save you, for from him do you proceed and come to us."[10] Pius XI noted in *Rite Expiatis:*

Strengthened, therefore, in the power of the virtues . . . Francis was singularly destined to reform and save the world of his day, as well as to give similar support to the Church. Twice in the church of St. Damian, where he used to pour out his heart and sorrows in

prayer and solitude, he had heard that voice from
heaven: 'Go, Francis, repair my house.' While Francis
misunderstood what Church it really meant, being
too humble to consider himself fit for such a great
undertaking, Innocent III saw more clearly into the
merciful plan of Providence, since he had a vision of
Francis holding up the crumbling church of the Lateran with his shoulders.[11]

Francis' whole life was a life of penance, a response of
created love to uncreated love. Everything he said and
did was permeated with his love for God and his People.
Because God had, in the first place, shown his tremendous
love for man by giving his Christ to the world, Francis
wanted to make a return of that love by living in the Spirit
of Christ, imitating him as much as he was able. Cajetan
Esser says:

> St. Francis had but one thought, one ambition after
> his conversion: 'to observe the holy gospel of Our Lord
> Jesus Christ.' But to him the Gospel was not merely a
> law or external norm on which to model his new life.
> What he wanted was to assume personally and con-
> cretely the life of Jesus — to imitate that life, both
> *human* and divine, with complete fidelity and sim-
> plicity. This imitation of Christ was for St. Francis,
> the very essence of the 'life of penance.' It is realized
> to the extent that man co-operates with Christ's sav-
> ing grace and exchanges his own servitude for God's
> freedom. To follow Christ meant to offer no resistance
> to God's saving activity, so that his grace and love
> can give themselves unstintingly to man and freely
> unfold with him.[12]

Since it was Christ, through his Spirit, who lived through
Francis, all the virtues were, in one way or another, evident in the Poverello's life. The popes have elaborated upon
many different ones. All of them were like many mirrors,
reflecting a brilliant light which, for Francis, was the spirit
and life of Christ.

Of all the popes, Pius XI elaborated most on the various
virtues. Pius XII emphasized their role in the reformation
of man and society. In his two major addresses given to
the tertiaries on the Franciscan spirit, Pius XII developed
this theme extensively.

In 1945, after the war, he addressed the tertiaries of
Rome, showing how Francis, in his day, had the answer
to the problems which are so evident in our own age. He
said:

> To the thirst for gold and wealth, to the desire to
> parade luxury and vanity, Francis opposed impassion-
> ed love for poverty, making Poverty his spouse on the
> cross of Jesus Christ. To the mad love of pleasure,
> sensual enjoyment, and the evil it brings about,
> Francis opposed mortification and a great desire for
> suffering, crucifying himself to the world and bearing
> in his flesh the stigmata of Christ. To jealousy, venge-
> ance, discord, hatred, and all the other bitter triumphs
> of pride, Francis opposed the serene joy of universal
> love, of the charity and peace of Jesus Christ.[13]

Ten years later, he said much the same to another group
of tertiaries. Laying great stress on the fact that the Franciscan life is, at its root, the complete imitation of Christ,
he pointed out:

> From this imitation of Christ there arises that Francis-

can poverty which flees from luxury and which loves particularly those things that give less pleasure to the eye and to vanity. From this is born Franciscan simplicity which brings the soul to search for God directly, following the short way, the simple way, that is to say, paying less attention to one's own disfigurement and more to the infinite beauty of God. From this springs Franciscan renunciation which is total and lasting, without rancor, bitterness, or begrudgement but, rather, made for the love of Jesus. From this surges up that candid Franciscan joy, which is not the same as noisy gaiety or unseemly laughter, but is rather the peaceful smile, full of amiable serenity.[14]

It is interesting to note how these summaries of Pius XII result in one basic virtue: peace, serenity. The life of penance lived properly in the Church always leads to and results in peace. Penance means turning to Christ, being filled with Christ — that Christ who *is* our peace, that Christ who is the King of Peace, that Christ to whose kingdom we belong.

Penance properly lived in the Church results in peace. More than this, it expresses itself in holy joy. Penance is the turning to God in one's heart. Joy is the shout of this God in one's heart. As Pope Paul said:

Because Francis, in a certain sense, lost himself in Christ, he found all things to such an extent that his heart sang with purest joy, proclaiming the ineffable gift of the divine friendship, the happiness of serving God, and the privilege of living in communion with the beauty of all creation.[15]

In Francis' life, penance could never be separated from

joy. Even though his whole interior being yearned to turn completely to Christ, even though his whole bodily frame was tortured with pain, joy became almost synonymous with his name. Francis was always the Troubador, the Herald of the Great King. In fact, as Pius XI pointed out:

> One of the most pleasing and joyous songs ever heard in this valley of tears is without a doubt the famous 'Canticle of the Sun' of St. Francis. The man who wrote this and the man who sang it was one of the greatest penitents. The Poor Man of Assisi who possessed absolutely nothing on earth and carried in his suffering body the painful stigmata of his crucified Lord was this man.[16]

In this penitential turning towards Christ there are three basic characteristics,[17] which the popes stress over and over again. We should investigate them a bit further if we are to understand Francis as they present him to us as a model. These three virtues, in their own way, are outward expressions of the life of penance. This means, as Pope Paul noted, that Francis imitated Christ internally "by forming his mind and heart in accordance with the thoughts and sentiments of the Gospel-Christ."[18] He witnessed to this externally in the virtues we shall study here. First there is *poverty*, the response to the "you," the leaving behind of earthly things to seize otherness in the embrace of Christ. With him, it means helping establish Christ's kingdom in one's own heart and in the hearts of all men. Then there is *charity*, the union with Christ, the Center of the universe, into the "we" of mankind. It permeates all our relations with our fellow pilgrims and strangers. It engenders a true spirit of simplicity towards everyone. Finally there is *humility*, that poverty of spirit in the "I", which makes

us realize our own complete nothingness before our God
and King. It makes us aware of our complete depend-
ence on him to continue the saving redemption of his Son.

THE POVERTY OF FRANCIS

Poverty is the badge of the order of the Poor Man. Leo
XIII wrote that it is its very foundation. Poverty is the
saving companion of all the People of God journeying toward the kingdom, especially of one who has embraced
it as his or her spouse. As Francis once said:

> Understand, my brothers, that poverty leads to salva-
> tion in a special manner since it is the nurse of humility
> and the root of perfection, the fruits of which are
> manifold though hidden. Poverty is the treasure in
> the field of the Gospel. To acquire it, we must sell
> everything, and what we cannot sell must be looked
> upon as cheap in comparison with it.[19]

There has not been a modern pope who has overlooked
the role of poverty in the Franciscan spirit. Poverty and
Francis are almost synonymous. Pius XI expressed his
views on the poverty of our Seraphic Father in the words:

> It is easier to imagine than to describe with what en-
> thusiasm he burned for evangelical poverty. . . . Christ
> our Lord, who 'was rich beyond our telling, . . . be-
> came poor for our sakes so that his poverty might
> make us rich' (cf. 2 Cor. 8,9). Francis had learned
> that divine wisdom which all the fallacies of human
> wisdom can never erase — that divine wisdom which
> has the power to renew all things with a holy newness.

> Jesus had declared, 'Blessed are the poor in spirit' (Mt.
> 5,3, Conf.) and 'If you want to be perfect, go now and

sell your property and give the money away to the poor — you will have riches in Heaven. Then come and follow me!' (Mt. 19,21). This kind of poverty, consisting as it does in the voluntary and deliberate renunciation of all things, undertaken upon the inspiration of the Spirit, is repelling to the unwilling, gloomy, and ostentatious poverty of certain ancient philosophers. Our Saint embraced this kind of poverty so heartily that he reverently referred to it as his lady, his mother, and his spouse. Referring to this, St. Bonaventure writes: 'Never was anyone so covetous of gold as he was of poverty; never was anyone more wary in guarding a treasure as he was in guarding this evangelical pearl' (*Leg. Maj.* c. 7, n. 1).[20]

Poverty: Identifying with Christ

In his usual thorough manner, Pius XI gives us the reasons why Francis embraced poverty as he did. First of all, it was to imitate the poverty of Christ. Then it was to emphasize the fact that this poverty of Christ had been forgotten by the world. "Francis loved Poverty so much," the Pope writes,

> because he regarded her as the companion of the Mother of God and of Jesus Christ, not just as the bridal companion claimed by him on the wood of the cross, but also as she was later forgotten by men and regarded as a bitter and unwelcome thing by the world. Just the thought of this used to bring tears and lamentations from Francis. Is it not touching to see a man like him being driven by his love for rigid poverty to such a degree that his former companions and many others thought him insane?[21]

Had they but known the true meaning of poverty and the other vows Francis would soon embrace, they would have realized its link with the very lives they professed to live as baptized members of Christ.

Truly, for Francis, poverty was the continuation of his life in Christ, of his baptismal vows. Pope Paul has said:

> The profession of the evangelical vows is connected with the consecration proper to baptism. It is, as it were, an act of personal consecration which completes the former. The individual dedicates himself wholly to God, making his entire life an act of service to him alone."[22]

How well these words apply to the Knight of Assisi who loved to serve his Liege Lord!

Just as Francis once renounced Satan and his evil works and pomps with *words* in baptism, so by his embrace of the vows he proved it with *deeds*. With his renunciation of himself, the "I", in baptism, Christ himself, the "you", invaded his life to be its sole treasure.

Poverty: Preparing for the *Parousia*

It was Christ (who redeemed the poverty of the whole world) who continued his poverty in Francis. Francis was the sign of this presence of Christ's poverty. By not being encumbered with the things of this world, Francis could live more freely as a pilgrim and stranger in it and as a citizen of the other world. Francis realized the world had been sanctified by the cosmic redemption of Christ; yet he knew it was still an imperfect beginning of the kingdom which would give way to that which was perfect. Poverty would help perfect the kingdom now. "Francis," Pius XI said,

while he commended and commended the practice
of this virtue to an exceptional degree in the rule of
the order, showed plainly how much he valued and
loved it with the words: 'This is that height of the most
sublime poverty which has established you, my dear-
est brothers, as heirs and kings of the kingdom of
heaven; it has made you poor in temporal goods, but
has exalted you in virtues. Let this be your portion,
cleaving to it completely, never desiring to possess
anything else under heaven for the sake of our Lord
Jesus Christ' (Rule, 6).[23]

In commenting on this passage from the rule, the Capuchin constitutions beautifully state:

Our Seraphic Father, St. Francis, contemplating
the most high poverty of Christ, the King of heaven
and earth, who, at his birth, could not find even a little
place at the inn; who, throughout his life, lodged like
a pilgrim in the houses of others, and who, at his death,
had nowhere to lay his head; reflecting moreover, that
in all other things he was most poor, and wishing to
imitate him, commanded his friars in the rule not to
possess anything of their own, so that, unencumbered,
like pilgrims of earth and citizens of heaven, they
might run with alacrity in the way of God.[24]

Such is the entrance fee to the kingdom of heaven which
begins on earth: that we free ourselves of attachment to
worldly things to turn our hearts to those of heaven. Such
a life of poverty consists not so much in being un-worldly
as being other-worldly.

The goal of Francis' life, union with God in paradise, so
stood out in his life that it colored everything he did. Having no attachment to the world, he could embrace it fully.

Everything in it was his, and he was Christ's, and Christ was God's. Here we find poverty bringing Francis to the summit of love and penance. Here poverty is spelled out in its true, literal meaning.

Poverty makes us ready at all times for the *parousia*, ready at all times to enter the kingdom with Christ. With it, we have already begun our heavenly existence. With it, our whole lives can be given proper focus in establishing attitudes toward the goods — or lack of goods — of this world. Pope John stressed this fact at Assisi when he visited the tomb of our Seraphic Father:

> It is St. Francis who has summarized in only one word how to live well, *ben vivere*, teaching us how we ought to value events, how to communicate with God and with our fellow man. This word gives the name to this hill which crowns the glorious sepulchre of the Poverello — Paradise, Paradise! . . . Dignity and holiness of life on earth is the sign of anticipation of paradise.
>
> The edifice of civilization rises on this and on no other foundation; by this, true greatness of practiced virtue and of sanctity desired with ardor, man is in a position to use the gift of freedom rightly so that justice might be realized and peace might be preserved and extended.
>
> From this height of a foretaste of paradise, life conserves the excitement of youth and is stamped with the mark of victory . . . Yes, venerable friars and lovable sons, paradise on earth is the moderate and wise use of the beautiful and good things which Providence has spread in the world for everyone's use.[25]

While reflecting on these truly powerful words of Pope John, one recalls that famous saying of St. Francis about money, "Let us beware that, having left all things, we do not forfeit eternal life for so worthless and mean a thing."[26] In Francis' eyes, everything has to be done in view of man's last end which has already begun. This means doing all to please Christ living in us and ruling in us. He himself has told us his kingdom is within us like a seed which grows until its final fruition is his *parousia*.

THE CHARITY OF FRANCIS

Because Francis put on the mind of Christ by stripping himself of all his "I-ness," Christ entered into his life with all his "you-ness." Christ's driving ambition which burned continually in his Sacred Heart was to cast fire on the earth, to bring all men to the love of God and the love of their neighbor. This became the ambition of the generous heart of Francis. The world had to be consumed, set on fire with the love of that God who had so loved it. It was Francis' vocation in the Church to light that spark.

Charity Springing from the Love of God

It was the Gospel message of penance all over again; the love of God must urge us on to win souls for his kingdom. "Today, as yesterday, Francis of Assisi remains an incomparable master of evangelical perfection, of that perfection which is nothing else than love and charity," Pope Paul has said. "This love and charity rises up to God our Father, in order to descend once more with all the greater force and ardor upon all men and all God's creatures."[27]

Christ said we will enter the kingdom by bearing witness to his love, as he bore witness to the love of the Father. He loved the world by serving it. Francis, true to the ex-

ample given him by Christ, became the lowest of all, serving as the least of all. He wanted it to be this way because Christ wanted it to be this way. For Francis, to serve
Christ in his people was to reign. To be charitable to them
was to serve Christ himself. This was the expression of his
childlike simplicity: he was a brother to everyone; he re-
spected others for what they were; he loved them. "From
this Franciscan way of imitating Jesus," Pius XII said,

> above all comes that universal charity which, because
> it sees everyone and everything in God, loves every-
> one and everything in him and for him, and which
> takes delight in everyone and everything because it
> takes delight in God.[28]

So noble was Francis' ideal of charity that Pius XI wrote,
asking,

> Who does not know that all this virtue had as its source
> and fountainhead the love of God? . . . This great love
> of God redounded upon his fellow men in such a way
> that he lavished help upon the needy, overcoming
> himself to such an extent that he singled out with spe-
> cial pity the miserably poor lepers for whom, in his
> youth, he had a natural horror. He devoted himself
> and his order wholly to their care and service. He
> wanted his disciples to love one another with a love
> no less than his own. Thus it came about that the Fran-
> ciscan family towered aloft 'like a noble edifice of
> charity in which the living stones, gathered from all
> parts of the world, were built up for a dwelling of
> the Holy Spirit' (1 Celano, n. 38).[29]

In Christ, Francis reached out to embrace the world. He
not only realized his own responsibility to attain the king-

dom of heaven or to have his sons attain it; he also realized
both he and his followers were committed to save all men.
They were, like Pope John in our day, to feel the heartbeat
of the world. Just as Christ laid down his life for the salvation of mankind, so would Francis and his followers spend
themselves for souls that they might be saved. This is the
underlying motive for his fraternal charity: Christ and his
love. As Pope Leo XIII wrote,

> Together with this love of the Cross, a most ardent
> charity invaded the heart of Francis. This urged him
> on to such an extent that he undertook the propaga-
> tion of the Christian religion and freely chose to ex-
> pose himself to the evident danger of death in order
> to promote his cause.[30]

With these words, Pope Leo has shown the reason for
the effectiveness of the Franciscan spirit in bringing about
the reformation of society. In Christ, all men are called to
salvation. This is why Francis went out to everyone. By embracing all men in general, Francis embraced each man
in particular. By embracing each man, he embraced the
whole man, body and soul, even though that man might
have been far from God. Truly, Francis' charity was the
universal charity of Christ.

Practical Expressions of Charity

Francis laid particular stress on various aspects of charity which did much to melt even the hardest of these
hearts far from God. One of these was his chivalrous concept of courtesy which flowed from the basic respect he
had for men redeemed by the blood of Christ. In this act of
universal redemption, Christ gave every creature a dignity
of inestimable value. Yet many had forgotten this fact

and neglected those without material possessions. This is why Francis devoted himself to them in a special way. This was his chivalrous courtesy. Pope Leo explained:

> His great charity embraced all men; yet the needy and downtrodden were especially dear to him. In fact, he seemed to delight in giving himself to those from whom others commonly fled or scornfully held aloof. In this way he did much to promote the ideal which viewed the human race as one family joined together in Christ.[31]

There has been no one in history as gracious, as courteous, as Christ. He gave of himself completely that he might help mankind not only in mind and spirit, but in body as well. Francis viewed this as courtesy. In his "Reminders" he wrote:

> Courtesy is one of the properties of the Lord, who serves out sun and rain and all his things which we need for our life, to the just and the unjust alike. For Courtesy is a sister of Charity, and she extinguishes hatred and keeps Charity alive.[32]

This same courtesy expressed so well in the life of Christ was witnessed to in the life of Francis. In action and practice, Francis showed mankind the graciousness and courtesy of Christ. He did this in the same way Christ showed it; by serving his fellow-men not only in the needs of their souls but in the needs of their bodies as well. He realized Christ and his Gospel had to enter men's souls through their bodies.

In acting upon this principle, Francis imitated the ideal of John the Baptist. John the Baptist was insistent on preaching the need of one's internal *metanoia,* one's internal turning to God, through external deeds, by turning to God's people in acts of justice. For him (just as it would later be for Christ and Francis), social justice was the expression of one's inner *metanoia.* "So," we read in the Gospel,

> John used to say to the crowds who came out to be baptized by him,
>
> 'Who warned you, you serpent's brood, to escape from the wrath to come? See that you do something to show that your hearts are really changed!'. . .
>
> Then the crowds would ask him, 'Then what shall we do?'
>
> And his answer was, 'The man who has two shirts must share with the man who has none, and the man who has food must do the same.'
>
> Some of the tax-collectors also came to him to be baptized and they asked him,
>
> 'Master, what are we to do?'
>
> 'You must not demand more than you are entitled to,' he replied.
>
> And the soldiers asked him, 'And what are we to do?'
>
> 'Don't bully people, don't bring false charges, and be content with your pay,' he replied.[33]

Because Francis followed a similar program he was able to inaugurate a social reform of great proportions. Pius XII noted of him, "To jealousy, vengeance, discord, hatred and all the bitter triumphs of pride, Francis opposed the serene joy of universal love, of the charity and peace of Jesus Christ."[34] This he did by going among the outcasts

and the lowly giving them the few belongings he might
have. And when he had nothing else to give, he gave himself.

THE HUMILITY OF FRANCIS

No one will be able to fulfill the program of social reform
envisioned by Christ, John, or Francis if he is not truly
humble. No one can be any good to his fellow man, to his
God, or even to himself if he is not humble, for humility
means living the truth. This means being one's self.

Humility: Living One's Truth

In our associations with our fellow man only he can be
effective who is true to himself, who lives his truth. Because
Francis lived his truth, he was a success. By living his truth
he fulfilled his personality. He was what God had made
him and did what God wanted. By living his truth Francis
became truly free. Celano says,

> He was humble in dress, more humble in conviction,
> most humble in reputation. This prince of God was
> not known as anyone's superior except by this bright-
> est jewel alone, namely, that among the lesser he was
> the least.[35]

Wasn't this the reason why Francis called his brothers,
who were to love and serve each other and mankind,
minores? Wasn't it also the reason why he always wanted
them to consider themselves fit only for the lowliest of
places? Humility for Francis wasn't just realizing the truth;
it was becoming witness to the truth. It was living and
acting in that spirit of freedom which can only come from
truth. It was living as the sons of God. When Cardinal
Ugolino suggested that some of the friars become bishops

Francis made it clear that humility was the way his minorites should live. With all reverence to the good Cardinal, Francis replied,

> 'Lord, my brothers are called *minores* so that they will not presume to became greater. Their vocation teaches them to remain in a lowly station and to follow the footsteps of the humble Christ, so that in the end they may be exalted above the rest in the sight of the saints. If,' he said, 'you want them to bear fruit for the church of God, hold them and preserve them in the station to which they have been called, and bring them back to a lowly station, even if they are unwilling. I pray you, therefore, Father, that you by no means permit them to rise to any prelacy, lest they become prouder rather than poorer and grow arrogant toward the rest.'[36]

We may talk at great lengths about the poverty and charity of Francis, but if we forget his humility, the third characteristic foundation of his spirit, we have missed the complete meaning of Francis. Many believe that poverty is the essential characteristic of Francis. It does not seem that Pope Pius XI would agree. The poverty he sees as characteristic of Francis is poverty in spirit which is humility, for he said:

> The lofty concept and generous love of poverty which dwelt in the mind and heart of Francis was too great to be limited or completed by the renunciation of external possessions. For who can embrace and profess poverty like that of Christ our Lord unless he becomes poor in spirit and a little one through the virtue of humility? ... It was indeed his chief care to

bear himself meekly as the last and least of all men.
Thus from the very beginning of his more perfect life,
he eagerly desired to be the ridicule and scorn of his
fellowmen. Though he was the founder and father of
his lesser brethren, he wanted one of them to be his
superior and master that he might wait upon his wishes. And, as soon as circumstances permitted, he laid
down the supreme government of the order, despite
their pleas and prayers, 'in order to observe the virtue
of holy humility' and to remain, 'from that day till
his death, a subject, living more humbly than any of
the others' (2 Cel, n. 143).[37]

Francis knew the attitude of humility is the only way
to attain the mercy of God, who never despises the weak
and lowly of heart. Knowing his own faults, he could
never place himself above others, but rather, with the mind
of Christ, considered himself the lowest of all men. Thus
it was his constant ambition to lower himself before others.
As Pius XI says:

> He esteemed all other men very highly and accorded
> them every mark of honor, becoming 'among the sin-
> ners as one of them.' For he looked upon himself as the
> greatest of sinners, saying that if God had given to
> any criminal the mercy he had bestowed upon him,
> the criminal would have proven to be ten times more
> perfect, and besides he attributed to God in true
> measure whatever was good and praiseworthy in him
> as that which he had received from him.

> For this reason he tried hard to hide the privileges
> and favors which might win for him the praise and
> regard of his fellow men — especially the stigmata of

our Lord Jesus Christ, which had been miraculously
impressed upon his body. And if ever he was the
object of praise in public or private he not only
thought and declared himself worthy of contempt
and scorn, but even became oppressed with incredible
sadness which he showed in sighs and tears.[38]

Humility: Foundation of the Order

Further, the Pope points out how Francis made humility
the foundation of his order:

It is on this foundation of humility that he wanted
his order of the Lesser Ones to find its footing and
strength. And while he would again and again exhort
all his brethren in words full of marvelous wisdom not
to glory in anything, even virtue and heavenly favors,
he warned and even occasionally rebuked those of the
brethren whose work carried with it the danger of
pride and vainglory, such as the preachers of the divine
word, those versed in letters and the arts, and the superiors of the convents and provinces. One could go
on and on; yet in all this, one thing should be remem-
bered: that Francis, following the example and words
of Christ, injected humility into the order as its chief
characteristic, for 'he wanted his followers to be called
Lesser Ones, *Minores,* and the prelates of the order to
be called ministers, *ministros,* so that the words of the
Gospel which he had promised to observe might be
used and that his followers might understand that by
their very name they had come to learn humility in the
school of the humble Christ' (*Leg. Maj.* c. 6, n. 5).[39]

Chapter Four

CASTING THE FIRE

Francis was completely subservient to the wishes of the
Vicars of Christ. Throughout the years, no one has realized
this more than the popes themselves. Especially in the
realm of apostolic witnessing to Christ, Francis and his followers have taken up the mission in the Church given them
by the popes.

Because Francis was humble, he could build a strong
foundation for his apostolate since he was doing the will
of someone else. In his encyclical on Francis, Pius XI
shows effectively that, were it not for the humility of Francis and the guidance of the Holy See, the Franciscan apostolate would have no meaning:

> The seraphic man, clinging to his ideal of the most ab-
> solute poverty, proved to be so lowly and humble that
> even when he stood at the head of the order, he wished
> with genuine simplicity to render obedience to one of
> the brothers — yes, we may add, to them all.

> For this reason, our Saint freely and completely sub-
> mitted himself and committed his will, the noblest
> of the Creator's gifts to mankind, to the Vicar of
> Christ by a vow of obedience. Oh, how badly they

are mistaken, how far they are from recognizing the man from Assisi, who try to suit their own theories and errors by fabricating and portraying a Francis — it is scarcely believable — who chaffed under ecclesiastical discipline, who cared nothing at all about the teaching of the Faith, thus being a precursor and herald of that false liberty which, in so many forms, has been preached since the dawn of the modern era and from which such confusion has resulted in Church and State.

Let this Herald of the Great King, by his wonderful example, teach all our Catholics and non-Catholics alike, how closely he clung to the hierarchy of the Church, to the Apostolic See, and to the teachings of Christ.[1]

With these words, Pope Pius XI has summarized the apostolic reform of St. Francis leading to peace in the individual as well as in society. Francis had given himself to Christ in his Church; the will of the Vicars of Christ had become his will. Being reformed in mind and heart in this way of humility, Francis found peace. Wasn't it natural then, that to bring about this same peace in men's hearts became his driving ambition?

Francis realized he could accomplish this only under the guidance of the popes. He understood the important fact that it did not matter *what* his sons would do as much as how they would do it — under the guidance of the popes.

PREACHING PENANCE TO THE WORLD

Like the Poverello himself, the popes visualize Francis' mission in the Church as one of preaching penance in imitation of Christ that the dialogue of salvation might be continued in time. Francis had said,

Let us consider well our vocation, most beloved brothers, and bear in mind that God in his mercy has called
us unto the salvation not only of our souls but of many,
that we go through the world exhorting all peoples by
word and example to do penance for their sins and to
observe the commandments of God. Fear not if you
are looked upon as mean and contemptible and ignorant, but preach penance with courage and simplicity; trusting that the Lord, who has overcome the
world, will speak in you and through you by his Spirit
to move all to turn to him and to observe his commandments.[2]

This explains why the most apt title Pius XI could give
Francis and his sons was "the new messengers of penance."[3]

Undoubtedly, Francis continually exhorted his brethren
to preach the Gospel of penance by word, yet he stressed
even more, the popes point out, the necessity of preaching
by deed. The world would be led to salvation primarily
through the personal example each friar gave. According
to Francis, his followers were to live as a visual aid helping
the world to understand the law of Christ. "The Friars
Minor," he said so simply, "have been sent by the Lord in
these latest times to give examples of light to those
wrapped in the darkness of sins."[4]

Francis and his brethren would lead the world to penance; first by living it, then by preaching it. This would
be the way Francis would fulfill the command given him at
St. Damian's. Referring to this incident which can be considered the foundation of Francis' apostolic activity, Pope
Leo XIII wrote:

It was more than a human voice which Francis heard
in the church of St. Damian's saying, 'Go and repair

my crumbling house.' No less remarkable was the vision given to Innocent III wherein he seemed to see Francis holding up the tottering walls of the Lateran basilica with his shoulders. The importance of these marvels is quite evident: they showed that, not only in his day but throughout the future as well, Francis would be a pillar and support for the Christian community.

Francis eagerly threw himself into his mission. The twelve men whom he gathered together to be his disciples were like a humble seed which, under God's blessing and the guidance of the Supreme Pontiff, quickly grew to become a most plentiful harvest. Disciplining themselves in virtue according to the example of Christ, he assigned to them the evangelization of various places in Italy and Europe and gave certain ones among them the commission to cross over to distant Africa. Presently, poor, unlearned, and common as they were, they appeared before the people. At the crossroads and in public places, without relying on splendid surroundings or high-sounding words, they began to exhort the people to turn away from worldly interests and to think seriously of the future life.[5]

In a similar way, Pope Pius XII showed how Francis' apostolate of leading the world to turn to God in penance flowed from his inner love for Christ which urged him on:

The poverty of Christ does not shrink up the heart, nor does it restrict or darken the love of a generous soul. Rather it lightens the little crosses of life, gives a lightness of step to work and inflames one with zeal

in order to set the whole earth aflame with that fire
which the Redeemer came to enkindle on earth. Thus
the love Francis had for Christ made him a Herald
of the Gospel, an apostle and recruiter of apostles, a
peacemaker and father of the knights of peace and
goodness, *pace e del bene* proclaiming the kingdom
of heaven in Umbria, in Italy and Europe and throughout the world. His word was heard in Assisi, in the
valley of Spoleto, throughout the region of Italy; his
feet left their footprints on the streets of Spain, on
the sands of Egypt, Syria, Palestine, and the Adriatic.
People of different tongues and customs heard his
voice. . . .[6]

Again, showing the global scope of Francis' missionary
activities as well as that of his brethren, Pius XI wrote:

Francis, the man catholic and wholly apostolic that
he was, who marvelously paved the way for reform
among the faithful, devoted his own as well as his
order's most strenuous efforts toward the conversion
of the heathen to the faith and law of Christ. It is not
necessary to elaborate upon something so well known:
how our Saint, filled with the desire to spread the Gospel and to shed his blood for it, sailed for Egypt with a
few disciples and presented himself courageously
and boldly before the Sultan. And is not the calendar
of the Church a most splendid witness for the many
missionaries slain in Syria and Mauretania at the
very beginning and springtime of the order?[7]

So intense was his desire to convert the world to the
Gospel of penance, that Francis incorporated a special pro-
vision in his rule for those who wanted to go to the heathen.

Christ had said, "Go, preach the Gospel to all nations." Francis saw to it that he and his sons would proclaim it to the ends of the earth.

THE POOR: THE IMAGE OF CHRIST

Just as Christ loved all souls so did Francis. Like Christ, Francis had a special predilection for the little ones, the poor, the *anawim*. "It is well known," Pius XI notes,

> that he was inclined by nature to help the needy, being, as St. Bonaventure testifies, so full of courtesy toward them that, 'even then with his ears open to the Gospel,' he made up his mind never to refuse them an alms, especially when it was 'asked for the love of God' (*Leg. Maj.* c. 1, n. 1). But grace abundantly perfected his natural disposition. Thus we find him, driven on by the compelling impulse, one day being repelled by the sight of a poor man but yet, being touched with contrition, running after the beggar, mercifully and generously relieving his needs.[8]

Like Christ, Francis had come to heal those who were sick and needy. "In his love for the poor and the weak," Pius XII writes, "he was the poorest among the poor, for in them he contemplated the image of Christ. His love for the poor also made him the poorest of the poor because in this great valley of humanity there were more who were lowly and poor than were great and wealthy...."[9]

To insult one of these little ones of the kingdom of heaven was to insult the Son of God, for as Francis himself once said, "Who curses a poor man does an injury to Christ, whose noble image he wears, the image of him who made himself poor for us in this world."[10] To show how Francis' love went out to the lowest, the poorest of the poor, we need only recall his wonderful love for the lepers, the most despised of God's humans. For Francis, they were signs of Christ; each one of them was his *"brother Christian."*

FOUNDING THE ORDER OF PENANCE

Besides identifying himself with the poor in imitation of Christ, Francis also mirrored Christ by calling all men to perfection. He did this by establishing a means through which all men could reform their lives by embracing the Gospel life of penance in a way similar to the way he had embraced it: the Third Order of Penance. Summarizing the historical events leading up to this revolutionary and practical means of living the Gospel which Francis outlined in his "Letter to All the Faithful," Leo XIII wrote of Francis and his sons:

> The eager public flocked in crowds to hear them and repented of their misdeeds, forgetting injuries, settling their quarrels, and returning to peaceful living. It is incredible with what forceful attachment the multitude was drawn towards Francis. They thronged after him in huge crowds whenever he appeared on the scene. Often the entire citizenry of the towns and cities begged in a body to be taught in his school of life.
>
> On account of this, the saint instituted the organization called the Third Order, which was to be open to every walk of life, to every age, and to both sexes, without breaking family or household ties.[11]

Thus the Third Order "was born to satisfy this thirst for heroism among those who, having to remain in the

world, did not wish to be of the world."[12] In Francis' day
thousands found in it an effective way to achieve Christian
perfection. They realized that, as Pope Pius X noted, "the
Third Order is nothing else but the Gospel in its entire
perfection,"[13] and that for them "to be a Franciscan tertiary" meant "to be a perfect Christian."[14]

Pope Leo XIII, the father of modern Catholic social
thought, saw in the Third Order the perfect instrument of
social reform. As an order of penance in the truest sense,
it is a Church-approved means in which one could make
a fuller response in love to the love which God had shown
them in Christ. "The whole object of this order," the great
Pope wrote, "as it was instituted by its founder, is to draw
men to the imitation of Jesus Christ, to the love of the
Church, and to the observance of all the Christian
virtues."[15] Showing how the ideal of the Third Order of
Penance is to live the Christ-life, Pius XI once said, "The
spirit of the Franciscan tertiary is the apostolate of Christian life, Christian faith, and Christian peace carried about
everywhere, to every home, in every walk of life, in every
one of the various social institutions."[16]

No need to study history to see what a great influence
the Layman's Order founded by Francis had on the
political, economic, religious, and cultural levels of society. Realizing the power inherent in the Third Order, we
should heed the words of the popes begging for its rebirth
in our times that it might once again draw many souls to
the love of God. The fact that the spirit of the *whole*
Franciscan family is nothing but that of Christ should make
us understand that we all have much to offer to imple-
ment the renewal of Christian life and morals.

FRANCIS' MESSAGE FOR OUR AGE

Every modern pope has noted the similarity between our own age and the age of St. Francis. Every modern pope has seen in Francis the solution to the greatest problems which envelop society today as it did in his day. Leo XIII, the first of the modern popes, has shown this in his powerful words:

> It is plain to see that untold benefits have come to Church and State from this one man. Because his spirit, thoroughly and eminently Christian that it is, meets the requirements of all times and places, no one can doubt that the Franciscan spirit is wonderfully fit for our age. This is even more true from the fact that the milieu of our time in so many ways resembles that of his own. As in the twelfth century, so now divine charity is greatly decreasing; and no less sad is the lack of Christian sense of duty which has been brought on partly through indifference. With a great eagerness and with great efforts, so very many are spending their time running after the comforts of life or are in the eager search of pleasure. Lost in luxury, they squander what is theirs and covet what is others. Extolling the ideal of the brotherhood of man, they talk more about it than work to bring it about, for their motive is self-love. Thus genuine charity toward the helpless and needy is vanishing by the day.
>
> In those days, the manifold errors of the Albigenses aroused the people to rebellion against ecclesiastical authority and disturbed the civil order at the same time, paving the way to a kind of socialism. Similarly in our own day the promulgators and propagators of naturalism have increased, who persistently deny the

duty of obedience to the Church and gradually reaching out beyond all right reason, harass civil authority as well, stirring up violence and sedition among the people urging confiscation, giving way to popular passions, and sapping the foundation of domestic and public order.[17]

As Francis had the answer for the troubles of his day, so do we: penance. Penance viewed as the turning to God in love is the only answer, for in turning to God we must turn to his people, in body and soul. Pope Paul VI has said that St. Francis was "one of the most original saints in the Church's history," because "he knew best how to express and live a harmonious relationship between the natural and supernatural, between the temporal and eternal."[18] This same task is incumbent on his followers. We must live a natural and supernatural life in time to achieve eternity which has already begun. We can do this by imitating our Seraphic Father.

> How many have followed his footsteps! How many have gathered under the steeple of the Portiuncula! How many virgins, with Clare of Assisi, have become his disciples! How many Friars Minor and tertiaries have followed after him![19]

Realizing our own times can be saved by the influence of Francis, Pope John urged, "The Franciscan spirit should be diffused everywhere. . . . It can be one of the most lively and laudable forces in obtaining the blessing of God for us."[20] This is also the mind of Pope Paul. According to Doctor Frederick C. Grant, an Anglican Observer at the Second Vatican Council, the Pope has "an intense interest in the life and the works of St. Francis."[21]

The life and works of Francis should be *our* inspiration,

as it has been the popes' inspiration, in making the ideals
of the Poverello come alive again in the spirits of men.
This should be the conviction urging every son and daughter to commit himself and herself entirely to Francis' spirit
with a heart full of generosity. As Pope Pius XII said so
forcefully,

> Society has an urgent need of this spirit, not only for
> its peace, happiness, and prosperity but, in way, for
> its very existence. It is for you, sons and daughters
> of St. Francis . . . to make that spirit sparkle and ra-
> diate.[22]

Again he declared:

> Today we freely and publicly admit that our great
> trust and hope rests on your order. For the generous
> spirit of the great St. Francis and the all-embracing
> perfection of his rule and program of life can apply the
> proper remedy to the mortal diseases under which our
> difficult age is degenerating. . . . Through you, dearly
> beloved sons, may the great St. Francis return to the
> children of this earth — that angel with the sign of the
> living God (Apoc. 7, 2), marked with the wounds of
> Jesus Christ who burned with such immense love for
> God and man.[23]

To fulfill this exhortation ought to be the goal of every
true son and daughter of our Seraphic Father. This is our
mission as members of the Church of Christ. This is our
role in carrying on the dialogue of salvation. It is our vocation; it is our witness.

Part Three

REFORM AND
DIALOGUE WITH
THE WORLD

Chapter Five

REKINDLING THE SPIRIT

If the children of St. Francis are going to be true to their name, they must be revolutionaries. Their incorporation in the Mystical Body of Christ demands it. Their vocation in the Franciscan Order necessitates it. Their membership in the community of man requires it. No matter how one looks at it, we are called to be saviors, reformers of mankind. We are called to make all men citizens of the kingdom of heaven, the kingdom of God which Christ has come to establish on earth.

For years the popes have called upon the Franciscan family to accomplish this task of the reformation of society. They have looked upon us with our ideal of penance to be the instruments of this reform. They have seen that our life is eminently fitted for this task. By individual renewal we will renew society. They have told us to look to our Seraphic Father for our inspiration in translating his message into a dynamic ideal for our age. His spirit must be our spirit, his ideal must be our ideal, his apostolate must be our apostolate. "Above all," Pope Pius XI wrote,

> let the image of the holy father and founder be re-
> flected in the three orders of his children[1] in which,

spread as they are 'throughout the earth's wide orb,'
as Gregory IX wrote to the Blessed Agnes, daughter of
the king of Bohemia, 'the Almighty is daily glorified
over and over again.'[2]

The image of Francis which we are called to reflect is the
same image Francis reflected, the image of Christ presented to us in the Gospels. "The Little Poor Man of Assisi
was truly the man of the Gospel — the Gospel rediscovered,
loved, and lived to the letter," Pope Paul said to the Franciscans.

> All those, therefore, who regard his spirituality as their
> own, all the members of his religious family, must go
> back to the very sources contained in the Gospel to
> carry out their ardent desire to renew the spirit of and
> conformity with Christ.[3]

ADAPTING TO THE NEEDS OF THE TIMES

To live the Gospel demands continual meditation on the
gospels. Yet it demands something more. In order to re-
incarnate Francis in our day, his Gospel-spirit must be
adapted to the needs of the times. This task is incumbent
not only on the individual Franciscan, but the entire five
branches of the Franciscan family.

When we stop being concerned about making Christ
relevant to the times, we have stopped being Franciscans.
There can be no thought of letting others do the adapting,
whether these "others" be members of the Franciscan family or institutes apart from the Franciscan family. If we are
to produce fruit in the Church, the *whole* Franciscan family, in all its members, must be renewed and must be the
instrument of renewal. As Pope John wrote to the ministers
general of the four obediences,

The very diversity which God allows to exist in the
Franciscan religious institutes should impel you to
exercise that zeal of which St. Paul speaks so highly:
'Be zealous for the better gifts' (1 Cor. 12, 31, Conf.).
The glory of the olive tree is its branches and the
glory of the branches is the tree — if these each truly
grow strong and nourish their olives with their sap.[4]

Many see no need for adaptation in an order, congregation, or society to make the message of Christ relevant to
the needs of the times. Many outsiders thus see no need
for that order, congregation, or society. Cardinal Suenens
notes in his now famous *Nun in the World* (whose message
is basically fit for the whole Franciscan family),

It is an undeniable fact that the wind of defeatism is
blowing about the older, traditional congregations. It
is widely held that they are all condemned sooner or
later to extinction, that history has already passed
them by, as has happened to so many previously flour-
ishing congregations. . . . It is no exception to hear it
maintained, even in our own Christian circles, that this
is the hour of the secular institutes or that the world
needs entirely new forms of the religious life.[5]

Few are pessimistic enough to agree whole-heartedly
with this conclusion, including the Cardinal himself. "Today, as never before," Pope Paul wrote in an apostolic exhortation on post-Vatican II life in the Church, "the
Church has need of the public and social witness that is
given by Religious Life. . ."[6] Though this is very true, there
is little doubt the critics do have at least some grounds for
their complaints. They know what has been accomplished
by the orders in the past and, with all devotion to their

glorious past, truly desire to see these orders accomplish their modern mission in the Church in a similar way, in a manner they feel their founders would have done. To say that such men are biased, uninformed, or ignorant would be wrong. Many are very learned and informed. They fully realize that the religious institutes have been called upon by the Vicars of Christ, especially Popes Pius, John, and Paul, to express the spirit of their founders in new relevant ways.

We are living members of the Church. We must renew ourselves continually; we must live in the modern world to save it as the popes would have us do and as Francis would have us do. Pope Paul, while still Archbishop of Milan, said, "Let us be clear on the point: the apostle is a shepherd, a fisherman; that means that he adapts himself to all the conditions of the goal to be attained, which is to win back souls and lead them to Christ."[7] Likewise Cardinal Larraona said to a group of religious superiors:

> All founders were pioneers and precursors . . . They accomplished what they did, and in the manner in which they did it, because this was an obligation imposed on them by the grace of God and the realization of their vocation, which was for them a keenly felt reality making an indelible impression upon their souls. By doing today *what* they would do in our place, what they would do if they were living in our times, we shall continue their work. They live; they have a right to live in us; and we have the sacred obligation of filial fidelity to carry on their work and live in their spirit.[8]

We must carry on their work in their spirit. We must live in these times, yet reflect other times. This expresses the principle of life itself. Something must always remain in an organism which is continually adapting to external situations. In the words of Pius XII to the Capuchins in 1948,

> Life itself calls for the alliance of the old with the new. It is by the joining of the two that life endures and retains its vigor. For this reason you must preserve intact and inviolate the ancient ideal from which you derive your origin and your special mission in the Church.[9]

In the same speech the pope stated that a life which reflects the times of Francis must also be adapted to the present. He also made it clear that in adapting to the present, we must never lose his spirit.

> Nevertheless, it must always remain your firm conviction that when you engage in these intensive activities of the apostolate, which this new age also demands of you, you must in no way weaken, much less radically change, that mode of life which is proper to your profession.[10]

In a similar vein, Pope Paul said to a group of religious which included the Capuchins:

> As far as new projects and undertakings are concerned, avoid those which do not fit in with the specific work of your order and the mind of its founder. A religious institute can retain its vitality and strength only as long as the spirit of its founder survives intact in the order's discipline, work, and the members' conduct.[11]

Adapting through the Words of the Popes

This is the period for decision. The Franciscan family has always gloried in its inspiring obedience to the popes. We cannot fail here to make our commitment to act upon the popes' words. We realize the truth of the words of Pope John and certainly want to be a *success* in the way he points out:

> The history of the Church, when studied without animosity, provides a very exhaustive documentation of two things; how, on the one hand, success adorns the life of religious orders when they preserve a pure and simple obedience to the Holy Church; and how, on the other hand, disadvantage and desolation, lamenting and weeping, befall them when they pursue, either alone or collectively, the paths of insubordination and lax discipline.[12]

We must be subject at the feet of the Church if we are to be effective, if we are to continue in existence. As long as an order maintains the spirit of its founder, it will have life and meaning in the Church. The spirit of our order images the spirit of the Church. It has meaning only in and through the Church. Gabriel Buescher says,

> It follows as a logical corollary that religious institutes, having a unique position in the Mystical Body of Christ, must of necessity be subject to the same organic laws of life which characterize the Body as a whole. We have already noted that the Church as a living organism is ever growing and developing, is ever renewing its interior life and adapting itself in its exterior life to the needs of every day and age. If religious institutes fail to renew continually their original spirit or to adapt themselves to the needs of the age, they will soon become fossilized members of the Church Militant unable to serve the purpose for which they were founded.

Sad to relate, whenever an institute lost sight of its original ideals or insisted upon maintaining customs and practices which were serviceable only to past generations, a gradual decline and ultimate death were the final outcome. With a degree of truth it can be said that many of the modern institutes have sprung up to meet the challenge of the present age when some of the older religious orders and congregations in the Church have failed to adapt themselves to modern needs.[13]

Today in the vocation crisis plaguing the institutes in the Church we do well to study these words. One comparative statistic shows the modern appeal of the newer forms of religious life. Between 1952 and 1962 the *combined* branches of the First Order and Third Order Regular, which constituted the largest institute of men in the Church, increased by five thousand members. During the same period, the Salesians, who have been in existence not much more than one hundred years, have increased by four thousand five hundred, surpassing the Capuchins in numbers.[14] Also during the same period, beginning with its *foundation* in 1952, the secular institute, Missionaries of Mary Immaculate, grew to one thousand members.[15]

To adapt we must study and be *aware* of the needs of the times. Pius XII noted in his address to the International Congress of Religious:

It has often happened that the founding fathers of religious institutes conceived new works by which they might meet the rising challenges facing the Church and her works. Thus they harmonized their enterprises with their times. Therefore if you want to follow in the footsteps of the example of your predecessors, in the

way they themselves acted, act as they acted. Examine
thoroughly the beliefs, convictions, and conduct of the
contemporaries among whom you live and if there
are some which are good and proper, make these
worthwhile features your own; otherwise you will
never be able to enlighten, assist, sustain, or lead these
people of your age.[16]

Further specifying the way this can be accomplished in
the various institutes, the Pope said:

There are some who think, perhaps correctly, that
three marks distinctively characterize the inclinations
and tendencies of our age; namely, broadness of vision in thought and deliberation, unification in plans
and arrangements, and speed in execution. Are not
these things also characteristic of the Gospel? Can you
not see that they are to be characteristic of those who
profess the Catholic faith and live it?[17]

If these counsels are to be followed, the various Franciscan institutes will have to be willing to grant necessary
freedom to their members that Christ's work may not be
impeded by secondary rules, formalities, or traditions reflecting by-gone days. If these do impede the work of the
members it will be only natural that a decline in vocations
will result. What Pope Paul VI said to the Capuchin superiors in 1963, who mentioned the lack of manpower to fulfill the needs of the Church, applies to all Franciscans:

This brings up the question of vocations. I hope your
order will abound in vocations. But to attract them
you must put aside all those things which can repel
the youth of today. You must go to them, associate

with them, without, of course, any compromise of principles.[18]

The order which has been noted for its freedom of spirit ought to continue that glorious heritage. By so doing, it can be an example to the whole Church.

Each Franciscan, then, must be a mirror of Francis to all other religious and dedicated laymen by continually renewing his spirit. Each Franciscan must also be a mirror of Francis by adapting his spirit to our times. Pius XII said to the Missionaries of the Kingship of Christ, the Franciscan secular institute:

> You have had access to this fire, to the flame of the love of Christ which burned beyond comparison in the Saint of Assisi. Therefore, we beg and exhort you with insistence, beloved daughters, that what the sons and daughters of the Seraphic Father did in the thirteenth century you might do at this time with the same spirit, even though the circumstances are certainly almost entirely different.[19]

We must mirror the times of Francis by *living* his spirit in our times. Can we be satisfied merely to look to the past, exalting the glories of Francis? We are called to be witnesses to Francis as Francis was a witness of Christ. The very meaning of the word "witness" demands that we show in our lives the reality we stand for. Thus by now, every Franciscan should have realized that it is his very vocation not merely to look to the life of our Father, but rather to make Francis' life his own in our milieu.

In his encyclical on Francis, Pope Pius XI stressed this necessity, using the words from the Roman Breviary:

> Whoever is charmed by the virtue of a saint, let him

be no less charmed by his studied service of God; and
therefore if he wishes to praise him, let him either
imitate him or cease praising what he is unwilling to
imitate.[20]

Adaptation is incumbent on both superiors and subjects.
Up to now we have stressed the need for proper adaptation
on the part of superiors. There is an equal necessity on the
part of subjects.

This brings up the question of obedience. In our age the
obedience which showed forth so clearly in the emptying of
Christ and the childlike simplicity of Francis is considered
by many as a hindrance to the freedom of the sons of God.
What Pope Paul VI wrote of the Body of the Church in
Ecclesiam Suam, applies equally well to us, an organ of
the Church:

> The Church will rediscover her renewed youthfulness
> not so much by changing her exterior laws as by in-
> teriorly assimilating her true spirit of obedience to
> Christ and accordingly by observing those laws which
> the Church (in our case the order as well) prescribes
> for herself with the intention of following Christ.
>
> Here is the secret of her renewal. Here is the secret
> of her *metanoia.* Here is the secret of her perfection.[21]

We who profess to "observe the Holy Gospel of our Lord
Jesus Christ," must realize the important word is "observe."
The mind and actions of Christ must be truly predicated
of us. This summarizes the only way we will reform the
world, by truly reforming our lives in imitation of Christ
and Christian principles.

In our sincere desire to renew our life there is always the
danger that we may be guided by faulty norms. In *Ec-*

clesiam Suam, Pope Paul makes references to some of these:

> Naturalism threatens to render null and void the orig-
> inal conception of Christian life. Relativism, which
> justifies everything and treats all things as of equal
> value, assails the absolute character of Christian prin-
> ciples. The tendency of overthrowing every restraint
> and inconvenience of life finds the discipline of Chris-
> tian asceticism burdensome and futile.[22]

Although we should be on our guard against such inter-
pretations, we must never be satisfied merely to abide by
the *status quo*. The popes want us continually and sincerely
to probe deeper into our life so that a dynamic image of
the Church might be reflected in us.

Adapting through the Liturgy of the Church

There can be no Franciscan spirit apart from the spirit
of the Church which is gained by following the counsel
of the popes. Likewise there can be no Franciscan life
apart from the life of the Church. The late Prefect of the
Sacred Congregation of Religious once said:

> ... it is in the Church that this life is lived, because
> it is in the bosom of the Church that we have made our
> three vows of religion; and it is of that Church's sanc-
> tity that each one of us should be a faithful and per-
> severing witness.[23]

Franciscan life is inseparable from the life of the Church.
To live the life of the Church means to live her liturgy.
The Church is the extension of Christ in time; the liturgy
is the continuation of His redeeming acts. It is man's loving
response in Christ to the God who has first loved us.

The liturgical movement is not a new idea in the Church. It is an attempt to return to the true font of Christian life, the center about which Francis founded and built his entire order. As Pope Paul views it, quoting *Mediator Dei:*

> The teaching of the Church, on the contrary, puts the liturgical renewal in its rightful doctrinal place, promotes it, and proclaims it as a reinforcement of the authentic exercise of the priesthood of Christ in the Church, as a necessary action, interior and exterior, of authentic Christian spirituality, as the worship having 'the greatest efficacy in achieving sanctity' and 'superior in excellence to private prayers' (*Mediator Dei,* Nos. 26, 37).[24]

For a Catholic, there can be no salvation outside the liturgy, for it is the primal source of grace. For the Franciscan intent on the imitation of Christ, there is no better means than the liturgy, the renewal of the salvific acts of Christ.

The popes have not yet made any major statements to the order as such to re-orientate itself around the liturgy in imitation of Francis. However, they have said many times that the liturgy is the foundation of Christian life. They have also told us to renew the spirit and life of Francis in our lives. This is why it is so important that we renew our lives in the liturgy. Francis *lived* the liturgy; so must we. In the words of Cardinal Suenens,

> One must start by putting in a class of its own the supreme meeting which daily unites God and man: the holy sacrifice of the Mass and the Communion which is its culmination. This is obviously the peak of

the spiritual life of religious. All that has been done to bring before the laity the value of the Mass is eminently applicable to nuns. Their piety must nourish itself at this primal source. The liturgical revival is as much a boon to religious houses as it has been for the laity: they cannot remain outside it, for their own sakes. . . .[25]

In his Lenten Pastoral of 1958 while he was still Archbishop of Milan, Pope Paul wrote:

Beyond doubt, our spiritual life stands in need of renewal, of improvement.
The spiritual decadence of our times demands it.
The cultural development of our people demands it.
The inner vitality of holy Church demands it.
The teaching authority of the Church demands it.
The eternal bidding of Christ, 'Do this in memory of Me,' demands it.[26]

By centering our lives around the liturgy, as the Vicars of Christ desire, we will be living the Gospel; we will be putting on the mind of Christ himself. His Spirit will form him in us and through him we will be able to revitalize our milieu. It is in the liturgy that we hear the Word of God, the law of the New Covenant which must inform and reform our whole lives, the law of love. It is also in the liturgy that we seal our part of the covenant of love by partaking in the feast of mutual love.

To reform society, we must first reform ourselves by becoming inflamed with divine love. By living the liturgy, with its "stupendous formative capacity,"[27] to use the words of Pope Paul, we will fulfill the Franciscan plan of penance and social reformation which will draw the world to the kingdom of heaven. In us Christ will draw men to himself as he promised. In us he will offer them to God who first loved us. Such is our role in the dialogue of salvation.

THE POVERTY OF THE FRANCISCAN

Franciscan life means a loving response in Christ to God's loving goodness for us. It is a *metanoia,* a turning to God in love, in order to be true citizens of the kingdom of heaven. This, as Pope Pius XII said, is the characteristically Franciscan way of imitating Christ.[28] Christ showed his love for us where poverty was in evidence, in the Crib, the Cross, and the Altar. The Franciscan therefore, will want to make a return of love through a similar emptying of himself. It was "this total surrender to the Christ of the Gospel that fashioned the very depths of the soul of Francis,"[29] Pope Paul said. This the follower of Francis can express in a complete giving of himself to Christ. This he can express in his detachment from the things of this world in his poverty.

Poverty: Other-Worldliness

Poverty for the Franciscan is not a matter of being unworldly, but rather other-worldly. If our treasure lies in heaven so will our hearts. Pope Pius XII links love and poverty. He said to the Capuchins:

> . . . so that you may be enkindled with that seraphic love for God and neighbor, with which the Patriarch of Assisi was aflame through the course of his whole lifetime. . . it is necessary to be penetrated and vivified all the more with the spirit of the Gospel so that you may shine with the splendor of poverty according to the spirit of your institute, that you may excel

by captivating simplicity and humility and especially that you may excel in that austere discipline according to your own traditional pattern.[30]

Poverty is the key to the effectiveness of the Franciscans in the Church and therefore, the key to the effectiveness of the reform of society. "In as far as the brothers depart from poverty, in so much will the world depart from them, and they will seek," Francis said, "and not find. But if they embrace my Lady Poverty, the world will provide for them, because they have been given to the world unto its salvation."[31]

Poverty must always flow from one's interior otherworldliness. If we have passed over with Christ to his kingdom within us, however, it should be manifested exteriorly as well. Our external lack of attachment to persons, places, and things in this world should mirror our internal attachment to God alone. Here we find the wonderful paradox and true meaning of poverty: by leaving all we gain all. "Whoever intends to live for the Lord and to serve him perfectly," Pius XII said, "must be a complete stranger to the world."[32] By having our hearts centered in God alone we can use all things the world has to offer as instruments to love him even more.

Poverty: Living in the Twentieth Century

In these days of modern adaptation, many believe there is little chance to manifest the fact that our hearts are centered in God alone. Because they feel there is so little chance to manifest this internal poverty, some content themselves by referring everything regarding poverty to their superiors. What the superior provides (or is asked to provide) is looked upon as coming from the hand of God.

This is certainly the proper view.

However, the individual must still regulate and establish norms for his or her expression of poverty as well. The superior cannot be the panacea for one's personal poverty. As Pope Paul stated:

> It is not enough for them to rely upon the judgment of their superiors regarding the use of goods. They themselves should be content with the basic necessities of life, shunning conveniences and luxuries which undermine religious life.[33]

Besides those who look to their superiors to answer the problems of living poverty, there are those who truly believe that, in our present situation, there can be no other expression of poverty than to live in its spirit. Although this is, to an extent, true, we must realize that one cannot *live* in the spirit of poverty unless he truly *dies* to material goods. One cannot lead souls to the life of penance, of turning to God, unless he is poor himself. We cannot point out the kingdom of heaven to men unless we have first sold everything in order to obtain it. We must bear witness in our lives what we preach with our lips. Pope Pius XII stressed this fact in his address to the Capuchins in 1948:

> What your glorious forefathers proposed for themselves, their companions and their future disciples, holding to it with all their powers, was evangelical poverty according to the law and example of the Patriarch of Assisi. . . . A wonderful remedy for the world's troubles and corruption is the example of evangelical poverty. Poverty is the companion of the God-given command of work. She is the friend of the virtues, the teacher of the people, the defense and glory of the

higher hope. Her noble banner has been placed into your hands. Preserve it without stain. It would be wrong to make a profession of poverty with the lips and heap contempt upon her with deeds.[34]

Lip-service is not enough. The Franciscan must be moderate in everything he uses and in everything he does. The barefoot friar, the sister with the patched habit, the tertiary with the moderate fashions, the pilgrim and stranger, should feel out of character in worldly pleasures and out of place in worldly dwellings. This applies to the friaries of the Franciscan institutes of men and the convents of the sisters as well as to the homes of the tertiaries and members of our secular institutes.

Prudence must be used; yet we must be on our guard against rationalizing excessive comfort, for as Pius XII continued, referring to our dwellings:

It may happen that some religious institute, because of development and progress, needs more and larger houses. It is right to provide for them, but in doing it, the proper measure and moderation must be preserved. Let glorious poverty which is symbolized by the habit and attire not be hidden in the shadow of sumptuous buildings or belied by the ease and comforts of their furnishings.[35]

The Franciscan should never allow himself to be truly comfortable in this life; his comfort can only come in the embrace of Christ. There is probably nothing so unrealistic or pathetic as a Franciscan who has allowed himself to be caught up in the pleasures of this world. He is betraying the very ideal he has embraced, the very thing to which he has vowed or promised his life. It is a pitiful sight for our

heavenly king. It is *unrealistic*. It indicates that one does
not realize that God has loved him, for if he did, surely
the only response he could make would be a similar return of love. Fathers Esser and Grau write, showing the
importance of poverty as love's response in the friars' lives:

> Because such total poverty is the answer of love, be-
> cause it leads the poor man to walk even as the poor
> Christ walked, in the path marked out by his foot-
> prints, it is a sure means of preaching the goal of that
> path. . . . If such is the importance of poverty in the
> life of the individual, of equal or even greater im-
> portance is its role in the inner life of the Church and
> indeed in the whole plan of redemption. . . . Hence
> the Friars Minor are called to re-present within her the
> saving and sanctifying power of her Head. As a result,
> they contribute more perhaps to the upbuilding of
> the Body of Christ by their poor life than they do by
> any external activity in the service of the Church.[36]

These are strong words. Only if we are poor ourselves
will we be true to our mission in the Church. If the people
to whom we preach poverty in spirit find friars or sisters
who do not truly bear witness to it, our message will be
in vain. By his life the Franciscan is to be the conscience
of Christianity; not a sign of contradiction. "For this reason," Pius XII said, "you must preserve intact and inviolate
the ancient ideal from which derives your origin and your
special mission in the Church."[37]

Poverty: The Witness to the World

If we are to save the world, if we are to return the world
to the spirit and practice of poverty as it was preached by
Christ in the gospels, we must be poor ourselves. This is

part of becoming *involved* in the Franciscan spirit. "That spirit is a spirit of mortification," Pius XII told the tertiaries of Rome,

> which consists in renouncing inordinate gratification, in resisting the appetite for pleasure, creature comforts and sensual satisfaction, in suffering all the annoyances and all the privations to which we may well say everybody is exposed in these difficult hours at every moment.[38]

This must be our life because, "only such a movement can lead back to faith in divine Providence and the love of Jesus Christ the great masses which have fallen victim to poverty and neglect."[39]

Pope John has said much the same: "It is only by an austere mode of life which puts into practice the poverty and self-denial taught by our Lord Jesus Christ, that the domestic and social order can decisively be moved toward truth, justice, and freedom. . ."[40] To the ministers general he wrote:

> Yours is not only the duty to flee from the sinful desires of the world, but also to show by your example as true sons of the Church, how sweet and desirable it is to worship God in true poverty, being content with little, going through life always joyful, going about doing good.[41]

Unencumbered by the things of this world, we can better draw all men to the next. Our joy in having nothing but Christ should be proof enough to ridiculers that whoever leaves everything, at least in spirit, receives the hundredfold, the peace of possessing all things in Christ. If the

world sees we have found happiness by detachment from
material goods and comforts, it will be led to imitate us.

THE CHARITY OF THE FRANCISCAN

Love for Others

Besides spreading an attitude of detachment from the
things of this world, the popes look to the sons and daughters of Francis to bring about harmony in the human race
by their love of the *men* of this world. This is part of the
Franciscan ideal of the brotherhood of all men which
unites the people of God in mutual charity. This, too, is
part of the Franciscan vocation in the Church, part of the
Gospel following of Christ. "The capacity to discover a
brother in every man, whatever his origin, state, condition,
or merits, is an exquisite and essential characteristic of the
Gospel teaching,"[42] Pope Paul once said.

The children of St. Francis, whose lives are centered
around the Eucharist, the center of unity and charity, will
understand they are responsible for the salvation of all
men. Thus they must love them as Christ did; for in Christ,
all of them are part of the universal "we" of mankind. Pope
Pius XII said the Franciscan spirit of charity "enfolds with
equal affection all people, all the classes, all the nations, no
matter how antagonistic they may be towards each other."[43]

Love for Each Other

Before we can show such a universal charity to the world,
we must first have a mutual charity among ourselves.
The world should be able to look to the Franciscans and
say of them, "See how they love one another!" Cardinal
Suenens says:

The religious community as such constitutes a "sign"

by which the Master ought to be able to make Himself
known; an apologetical sign of brotherly love lived according to Jesus' words, 'So they may be made perfectly one. So let the world know that it is thou who
hast sent me,' it is a fraternal community trying to
continue in the world the prototype of the primitive
Church described in the Acts of the Apostles: (4, 32-
35)....[44]

By showing the love they have for each other and for
all men, the Franciscans inspire men to love one another.
To show the world a living example of the charity of the
Son of God is an essential requisite of our vocation and one
of the noblest tasks given us by our Seraphic Father. In
speaking to the followers of St. Francis, it was the prayer
of Pope Pius XI that:

their Seraphic Father from on high who never ceases
to sustain and nourish the mystical vineyard which
he planted with his hands might now strengthen and
nourish his issue with the liquid of brotherly love so
that, 'being one heart and one soul,' they might devote
their energies to the reformation of Christendom.[45]

It is of the nature of charity to serve others in courtesy,
to look to their needs while forgetting one's own. It is also
of the nature of charity to spend oneself for others that the
love of God might blossom in their hearts. In the words of
Pope Pius XII, such Franciscan charity is

shown in harmony that is maintained with those
among whom you live, in condescension to them in
everything not contrary to the law of God, in the
exclusion of all contention and factions, in love that
is universal.[46]

At the root of this spirit is humility, a love placing others above oneself, a love of the "you" instead of the "I." In fact, Christ himself said that we show our love for our brothers by laying down our lives for them. This is nothing else than emptying oneself of one's own love by practicing the virtue of humility.

THE HUMILITY OF THE FRANCISCAN

Much has already been said about the humility of Francis. The need for humility in his followers has not changed through the ages. Just as Pius XI said that "It is on this foundation of humility that he wanted his order of Lesser Ones to find its footing and strength"[47] so did his immediate successor say to the children of Francis:

> Let your chief glory be true Christian humility which, coupled with courtesy and goodness, succeeds wisely in gaining the good will of men. They live in a world of darkness into which it is extremely difficult to enter. But the secrets of the human heart break down before humility. Only by it are they saved by the sweet triumph of certain victory. Such a victory has come to many saints of your order through this wonderful virtue — Felix of Cantalice, Lawrence of Brindisi, Joseph of Leonissa, Fidelis of Sigmaringen, Conrad of Parzham — to mention only a few.[48]

Humility: Service in the Church

Without humility, our life and apostolate will be barren. Humility is the true foundation for an effective apostolate. Humility, viewed as loving service toward God and man, *is* the Franciscan ideal. It is our apostolate too, for in the eyes of Pope Paul:

The fundamental program of an apostle ought to be to present to the world an admirable Christian witness primarily of our own mutual love for each other and then of the love we bear those to whom we desire to preach the Gospel. The great aim of the apostolate is not to be a conquest but service; not to be a movement motivated by self interest but by concern for others.[49]

Stressing the need for humility in his order to insure an effective apostolate, Francis said to Cardinal Ugolino:

If you want them to bear fruit for the Church of God, hold them and preserve them in the station to which they have been called, and bring them back to a lowly station, even if they are unwilling.[50]

Commenting on this saying of Francis, Fathers Esser and Grau write:

What they are called to be in the Church is Lesser Brothers; their mark, minoritas, littleness. From this alone must all their activity grow if the wish to fulfill that special mission for the kingdom of God to which the Lord has called them. That this holds true in equal measure for the sisters of the Second Order and for all Third Order brothers and sisters, should be self-evident.

If on the other hand, their activity, their apostolate, is not the out-growth of their minoritas, if they fulfill their appointed duties, even in the kingdom of God, in a way no different from other workers in the vineyard of the Lord, they no longer have any significance in the Church as a specific community or cell

in the Mystical Body and have forfeited their right
to exist. They should not be surprised then if the Lord
calls other individuals and groups to take their place
and accomplish the task and mission so urgent for
the inner life of the Church which should have been
theirs.[51]

Pope John himself has underlined the need for humility
in effecting a fruitful life in the Church and its mission
when he writes in his letter to the ministers general:

> Your Lawgiver and Father, poor yet rich, humble yet
> exalted, resembling Christ as no other man ever did,
> and being inflamed with seraphic ardor, wanted above
> all, as he showed by word and by the example of his
> life, that in observing the law of the Gospel, the foun-
> dation laid by our Divine Savior should ever stand un-
> shaken: 'Blessed are the poor in spirit, for theirs is the
> kingdom of heaven' (Mt. 5, 3., Conf.). If this prin-
> ciple is neglected, no good works or no fine words
> will ever bear fruit.[52]

CONCLUSION

Living a life of the love of God by living the liturgy of
the Church, the Franciscan best witnesses to the life and
spirit of Christ through poverty, charity, and humility.
Without these, the popes would have us understand, we
will lose our identity in the life of the Church. Without
these, we will lose our sense of mission, the sense of our
role in the renewal of society. With them, they tell us, we
will be at peace with the peace of Christ. With them, we
will best spread that peace to the world. Poverty is the
emptying of oneself to be filled with the peace of Christ.
Charity is the spreading of this peace to others. Humility

is the submission to Christ's mind that his reign as the Prince of peace might continue in us and that he might go on spreading his reign, his kingdom, in the hearts of the world. Such a peace can only triumph if we have turned our hearts to the King of Peace that he might take complete possession of them. There can be no true peace in our hearts or in the hearts of men unless Christ, the Author of peace, becomes our living peace.

Chapter Six

"THE WORLD HAS URGENT NEED OF THE FRANCISCAN SPIRIT"

The Franciscan reform has been one of the most effective instruments for peace in the history of the Church. Social peace, first of all, is an individual matter. It springs from a personal turning to God, from an individual's life of penance. One must live the life of penance which brings this peace, before he can spread peace to others. "In fact," Pope John wrote in *Pacem in Terris,*

> there can be no peace between men unless there is first peace within each one of them; unless, that is, each one builds within himself the order wished by God. This is why St. Augustine asks:

> 'Does your soul desire to overcome your lower inclinations? Let it be subject to him who is on high and it will conquer the lower self. There will be peace in you — true, lasting, well-ordered peace. In what does this order consist? God commands the soul, the soul commands the body. There is nothing more orderly than this.'[1]

Once the individual has turned to God and let Christ reign in his heart, he will want to spread that peace to all men that they also might be true members of the kingdom. This is the Franciscan outline for world reform. The words of Pope Paul to a German Catholic convention are to the point:

> God is renewing the world of today by the powerful changes of which we are permitted to be witnesses and jointly responsible. The Church may not be of this world, but she lives in it and has a mission for it. Therefore her members on earth are called to reflect upon the changes we are experiencing at the beginning of a new epoch, so that each person may start the spiritual renewal within himself. The spiritual renewal of each individual — his life from God, in God, and for God — is the basis for the spiritual renewal of the family and hence for the different nations.[2]

Pope Paul reiterated this same thought in his peace appeal at the United Nations, October 8, 1965.

Francis felt the world could not look upon his followers (whose poverty and humility were equaled only by their charity, joy, and peace) without realizing that "pleasures" other than those gained by fortune and power are available to those who seek them. This ideal of Francis fascinated the hearts of the people of his day and still draws the modern heart to God. In turning to God in love and the spirit of penance by leaving the things of this world, they allowed Christ to permeate their lives with his princely peace. The peace of Christ, the world discovered, was worth every privation. It alone surpasses human understanding.

Is this not the chief reason why the popes look to the children of St. Francis to establish world peace? A lengthy address given by Pope Benedict XV to a Secret Consistory

of the College of Cardinals shortly after he had written
his monumental encyclical on St. Francis can be cited as
a full development of the popes' thoughts on this matter.
Among other things, he especially stressed the fact that
Francis employed individual reformation as the means to
effect the reformation of society with the words:

> It is indeed a pleasure for Us to see your august body
> assembled around Us once more that We may speak
> with you on the interests of the Church and the good
> of souls entrusted to Our charge. We wish that We
> could paint a bright picture for you, but the sad state
> of things prevents it. In fact, the disorder and strife
> still prevailing in various parts of the world cause Us
> serious anxiety. In Our unfailing desire to do every-
> thing possible to remedy these evils, We have let no
> occasion pass by in which we could help society re-
> turn to peace and tranquility — that same tranquility
> which society frequently gained for itself in centuries
> past by listening to the Church. That is why We took
> advantage recently of the celebration of the seventh
> centenary of the Third Order of St. Francis to invite
> the whole world to that spirit of self-sacrifice and
> Christian charity by means of which the Patriarch of
> Assisi was filled with the desire to bring back souls
> to the love of God. In this way there was remedied
> in great measure the disorder of his times.

Indeed, never was there such need as there is today
of calling this poor humanity to the practice of self-
sacrifice and brotherly love; this poor humanity, first
scourged by war and now thrown into disorder by lust
of this earth and by political factions. Never was
it so necessary as it is today that the reformation of

the individual based on Christian lines should be raised to check effectively the paganism which is infiltrating every phase of public and private life.[3]

In these words, Pope Benedict reflects the thoughts of the modern popes admirably. All of them have found in our era a marked similarity to the age of St. Francis. Likewise, all of them have concluded that the same means he used to effect the renewal of society can be used effectively by us in our century. The words of Pope Benedict, spoken over four decades ago, still can be applied to the conditions of our age. These same words can be applied to the means we have to solve the tension of our age.

If it is true that the actual state of war has ceased, there still has not yet returned to families and to all social and national classes a sure and lasting peace, that tranquility and order which springs from the spirit of brotherhood and Christian solidarity. . . . But now it is evident to all that the rules of peace so laboriously worked upon by the most experienced politicians may, in fact, be written in treaties, but they can never become living realities, nor have strength or power, nor penetrate consciences unless, in the first place, they are based on the principles of justice and equality and, in the second place, there arise again in minds and hearts those principles which transformed the world from pagan to Christian and, in the day of St. Francis of Assisi, also healed and restored a society full of disorder and corruption.

Only with the control of one's own passion comes the interior order of the individual which is the base of the social order. Only by the practice of brotherly

love will there arise again the mutual trust among
social classes and peoples which is the font of true
and lasting peace. This is what We beg of the Divine
Goodness with our whole heart — that this Christian
renewal might be accomplished which will bring
peace and tranquility back to earth, hoping at the
same time that the centenary we have been celebrat-
ing may spread the spirit of St. Francis. . . .[4]

The popes cannot repeat it often enough: only the individual will be able to reform the whole. Only the individual
full of the peace of Christ will be able to spread it
effectively to others. This is the Franciscan apostolate.

PREACHING PENANCE TO THE WORLD

"In a sense," Pope Paul has written, "the apostolate and
preaching are the same. Preaching is the primary apostolate."[5] The Franciscan family exists in the Church, according to the minds of the popes, for one purpose: to call the
world back to God in the spirit of penance. This is best
accomplished, not so much by words, as by actions. Our
sermons are most effective when we witness, not when we
preach. "Even when you are silent," Pope John wrote
the ministers general of the order, "your whole life should
be itself a sermon. Everything in your behavior should
breathe forth a spirit of that solid faith, majesty, conti-
nence, and sincerity which you preach."[6] Francis himself
once said:

Since you speak of peace, all the more so you must
have it in your hearts. Let none be provoked to anger
or scandal by you, but rather may they be drawn to
peace and good will, to benignity and concord through
your gentleness.[7]

It cannot be repeated often enough that here lies the primary way we will turn the heart of the world to Christ. If the world does not see in us witnesses to the eternal truths we profess, it will never turn from its preoccupation with the things of this world.

When the popes mention the primary apostolate of preaching, considered essential to the Franciscan order, they stress the primacy of preaching by example.[8] We can lead souls to turn to God in love, they point out, only if we have done so first. If the love of God is in us, we can do all things. Nothing will be too hard, for at the foundation of our lives will be the peace of Christ urging us to proclaim the good news of salvation to all men of good will. This is what Francis did. Pope Benedict wrote:

> Burning with a seraphic love for God and man, Francis could not contain his charity within his heart; he had to pour it out upon everyone. Hence, though he began by reforming the private and domestic life of his followers and adorned them with Christian virtues, as though he might have seemed to want nothing more, still he had no intention to content himself with that alone. He used the reformation of individuals to be the means to arouse in the hearts of the people a love of Christian wisdom and to win all unto Jesus Christ.[9]

The words of Pope Pius XII addressed to the Capuchins many years later seem to be a direct commentary on what Benedict XV said about Francis:

> With a heart set on fire by divine love, sparing no efforts, enter into the midst of the multitudes as mediators of peace, teachers of truth, providers for Chris-

tian piety and holy religion. In all you do, shine before them by your example that you may more easily draw their souls to yourselves and thus to Christ. Only in this way, with the inspiration and help of divine grace and the resolve to emulate the glorious and holy deeds of your great forefathers, will you harvest the fruits of salvation in ever-increasing abundance.[10]

World Responsibility

For the Franciscan, the harvest of souls to be cultivated for salvation in God's kingdom spreads over the whole world and embraces all men. Francis realized his vocation was to be another Christ, to say with him: "It is fire that I have come to bring upon the earth — how I could wish it were already ablaze! There is a baptism that I must undergo and how strained I am until it is over!"[11]

Like Christ, Francis could not rest until he saw all men incorporated into the Kingdom, given over to the rule of Christ, sharing in his peace. As a member of Christ and, therefore, as a member of the universal "we" of the brotherhood of man, Francis felt keenly his responsibility to help all men reach their goal. He felt the necessity for all men to return to God in a true *metanoia* of mind and heart that Christ might reign in their lives. Our Seraphic Father is a perfect example of one who lived the following words of Pope Paul:

> All of us are responsible for our times and for the life of our brothers. We are responsible before our Christian conscience. We are responsible before Christ, before the Church and history; we are responsible before the face of God. Responsibility is a tremendous word

which only the saints with their intuitive optimism conceived with energetic force.[12]

It is our vocation to become saints with a true world vision, a true *Weltanschauung*. Pope John XXIII said, "By now every member of the Holy Roman Church is permeated by this fact: that insofar as he is Catholic, he is and considers himself to be a citizen of the whole world, just as Christ is the adored Savior of the whole world."[13] By the same token every Franciscan in the Church must be permeated by the fact that he cannot rest until all men are saved, until all men turn to God in love. Francis' apostolate embraced all men; so should ours. Evidently such a life involves more than the recitation of prayers. "We seek from Our beloved children not only prayers," Pope John insisted, "we also seek from them a *renewal* of Christian life."[14]

Establishing the Reign of Christ

In our work to renew Christian life, all our labors must be founded on Christ himself, for there can be no Christian life without the inspiration of Christ. His mind must be our mind. His ideals must be our ideals. His mission must be our mission.

Undoubtedly the Franciscans have committed themselves in a special way to making Christ's mission our mission. The Franciscans have spread to all corners of the world fulfilling the injunction of Christ, "Go, preach the Gospel to all nations." Today Franciscans are found in the missions of the Church throughout the world, as Francis envisioned. Noting this extensive missionary activity, Pope Pius XI wrote:

The numerous followers of Francis have carried on
this apostolate in the course of ages, even at a lavish
cost of blood, so that they are privileged by the Roman
Pontiffs in having the greatest number of heathen
territories assigned to their missionary activities."[15]

From the very beginning, the Franciscan family has had
as its driving force and inspiration the prayer of Christ
the night before he died — "That *all* may be one." The
family that is centered around the Eucharist, the bond of
unity, should naturally have this desire uppermost in its
mind. This is a spirit of ecumenism, the world-vision. It is
part of the Franciscan vocation. Just as the Christian vocation is essentially a missionary vocation, so is the Franciscan's. Just as the mission vision of the Christian must be
revitalized, so must the Franciscan's.

At the ceremonies marking the seven hundred and fiftieth anniversary of the approval of the Franciscan rule,
Pope John XXIII made a stirring appeal to the order for
such a revitalized mission spirit among its members. "What
can be said of this . . . fundamental attribute of every good
son of St. Francis?" the Pope asked:

> What can be said of that spirit of catholicity and
> apostolicity which St. Francis presented to his con-
> temporaries and bequested as a most precious herit-
> age to his friars, when he made it a precept of the
> holy rule. . .?

In his *Legenda Major et Legenda Minor*, St. Bonaventure devotes some touching pages to the preparation
for a vast missionary apostolate in accordance with
this precept. The precept had as its object the direction of the work of winning innumerable souls, a task

which, over the course of seven centuries, was to spread the knowledge of and carry out the triumph of the name, the love, and the reign of that wholly spiritual kingdom of the Crucified Jesus, the Savior of the world.[16]

Continuing this theme, Pope John warns us against complacency in the success of the past. He asks for deeds, not words; action, not academics.

The rich libraries in which precious volumes, both ancient and modern, record the deeds of the Franciscan missionaries and the shedding of their blood, should not be merely honored like so many laurels on which the heirs of such glory may rest; rather, rendered more vivid by the occasion of the centenary celebration, they should serve as incentives to 'strive after better things.'

This is one glory of the Franciscan family which should be, and in fact, is, laudably pursued in noble and holy rivalry. In this the Franciscans are united with the spiritual forces of other congregations, which today are undertaking with more vitality than ever before, tasks which have come up in some especially difficult and contested areas of the world.[17]

Our founder was an idealist. He wanted to embrace the whole world, rich or poor, brown or white, freedman or slave. He wanted to see all equal in Christ; not a classless society in the kingdom of man, but a classless society in the kingdom of Christ.

Francis was also a realist. Leo L. Dubois, S. M., treating the reform movement of our Seraphic Father, says of Francis' concept of the brotherhood of man:

Francis believed that the inequality of classes is necessary in any social order. 'The rich are our brothers,' he said once, 'for we have all been created by the same Creator. They are our lords, because they help us in doing penance by supplying to us what is necessary for the body' (LTC, n. 58).

Other reformers both before, and in St. Francis' time, had seen no other remedy for the abuses of wealth than revolt against the rich, and the extinction of class. Francis not only recognized the distinction of social classes, but confirmed it. In his Third Order, members of all classes were received without losing the privileges of their positions; kings and serfs belonged to it, but the kings remained kings and the serfs remained serfs.[18]

Such was the attitude of Francis toward all men, from the lowest to the highest.

Pope Pius XII spoke of his mark on the higher levels of society when he said: "In all succeeding centuries your Franciscan movement has provided means and incentives which even in our age have proved remarkably effective in developing Christian virtue especially among the influential classes."[19] We need only look to some of the members of the Third Order in recent times to realize this: Garcia Moreno, martyr-president of Ecuador; Blessed Contardo Ferrini and Vico Necchi, university professors; Eve Lavalliere, actress; Francis Thompson and G. K. Chesterton, poet-writers, Thomas Murray, member of the atomic energy commission, and Lena Edwards, Negro physician and winner of the United States' Freedom Medal in 1964.

THE POOR: THE IMAGE OF CHRIST

Though a great number of influential people have responded to the Franciscan ideal, history has proved that the Franciscan spirit has been most effective among the little ones, the *anawim*, the poor. Christ said: "Blessed are the poor in spirit." Referring to this, Romano Guardini writes, " 'Poor,' first of all, are the needy and despised of the world; but also those, however rich and honored, who recognize themselves as participants in the universal poverty of fallen creation."[20] The poor in spirit and the poor in material goods have a claim on the Franciscan. "The world is our mission," the Capuchin mission slogan has said; but it adds, "the poor are our special charge."

Francis gloried in making his apostolic presence felt among the lepers and the other outcasts of society. The Franciscan should glory in working with those abandoned by others, from whom he will receive no praise, and no honors.

Our mission is to be servants of the little people of God, the *anawim*, no matter where they may be, that the kingdom of God might bear fruit in their souls. What Pope Pius XI said of the Capuchins applies to all Franciscans: "Where conditions were at their worst and help was needed; in places abandoned, where no one else would go, there you will find the Capuchin."[21]

We live in an era of prejudice and bitterness, but also in an era of emergence. In all fields, on all levels of society, men are becoming aware of their enormous capabilities. They are discovering they are custodians of power. United in arms they can overthrow rulers; united in effort they can harness hurricanes or corrupt civilizations; united in love they can win the world for Christ. Among all these

people, the ones who are facing the most critical period
of their existence are the *anawim*, the little ones, the poor.
Is there anyone or any group more in a stage of emergence
than they? They are discovering they also have power not
only physical, intellectual, or moral but more important,
the power to *be*.

Stressing the fact that these people should be given
their "elementary human rights," Pope John wrote in
Mater et Magistra;

> We, therefore, who love all men as our sons, feel con-
> strained to repeat here very definitely what we made
> clear on another occasion: "We are all equally respon-
> sible for these undernourished peoples. [Hence] it is
> necessary to educate one's conscience to sense the
> responsibility which rests upon each and every one.
> . . . (Allocution, May 3, 1960, *AAS*, 52 [1960], p. 465)."

> In order that this obligation of helping those who are
> in misery and poverty might be happily carried out,
> the Church has always and vigorously declared that
> it should also be felt most strongly by Catholics
> because of the fact that they are members of the Mys-
> tical Body of Christ. 'We know and to some extent
> realize, the love of God for us,' St. John says, 'because
> Christ expressed it in laying down his life for us. We
> must in turn express our love by laying down our lives
> for those who are our brothers. But as for the well-
> to-do man who sees his brother in want but shuts
> his eyes — and his heart — how could anyone believe
> that the love of God lives in him?' (1 Jn. 3, 16-17).[22]

Not only the individual but also the community is to
identify with the poor. Pope Paul insists:

> Besides the practice of poverty on the individual level, one must not neglect the practice of it by the religious community as a whole. . . . Religious institutes should have due consideration for the social conditions of those who live around them. . . . The temporal goods which divine Providence has bestowed upon them should be used to alleviate the needs of their poorer brothers in their own areas and around the world.[23]

We may not always have the means to relieve the needs of the poor; still we can have a detached heart of mercy and compassion. These are the riches we can share, showing that the love of God lives in us as we share in their poverty.

The Emerging Poor

From Tokyo through Bombay to Johannesburg; from Mexico City through Rio to Santiago, millions created in the image of God in their souls and in the image of Christ in their bodies, as Francis once said,[24] are beginning to realize they are human beings after all. As Louis and Andre Retif point out in *The Church's Mission in the World:*

> The third revolution taking place under our very eyes, after the French Revolution and the working-class revolution of Marx and Engels, is that of the poor, of the 'third,' oppressed world living in subhuman conditions, the revolution of the peoples of those continents which only yesterday were under colonial domination. And it is a revolution which is quite different from its predecessors. Yet its evolution is linked with them although we cannot foresee in what direction its influence will be brought to bear. But the historical

context in which it is taking place is obvious for us to see and it involves the whole mission efforts of the Church.[25]

These poor throughout the world are impatiently emerging. The constant national revolutions by bloodshed in the poor nations and the constant personal revolutions by crimes in the rich nations evidence this fact. Little wonder, then, that the popes look to the Franciscans to enter into these areas, to reform society, to enrich the poverty of these poor by witnessing to the poverty of their Exemplar, by calling them to penance.

The popes ask us to intensify our "evangelical labors now that the needs are immeasurably growing"[26] among the poor. They know, however, that we can enter the souls and spirits of these poor only through their bodies. We must help provide first for their bodies, then for their souls. Christianity will not alleviate the world's misery completely. Still we must do as much as we can; by soup kitchens or living with the poor, sharing their life to win them for Christ, or admitting more of the poor to our hospitals, schools, and other institutions. Members of the secular institutes and Third Order can become actively engaged in seeking better living conditions for the poor.

Again, as Pope John also pointed out, in the missions we can co-operate with governmental agencies as he stressed in *Mater et Magistra*. We can work with the United Nations, the Peace Corps, or Alliance for Progress. We can also co-operate with private charities. At home, among the poor, we can cooperate with governmental agencies such as those connected with the War on Poverty. The sense of urgency should compel us to spend ourselves that the souls of the poor might not be lost. What Pope Pius

XI said in his encyclical on Communism, to the priests of
the world, applies to each and every Franciscan:

> In a special way We recommend to priests again, the
> oft-repeated counsel of Our predecessor, Leo XIII, to
> go to the workingman. We make this advice Our own
> and, faithful to the teachings of Jesus Christ and his
> Church, We thus complete it by saying: 'Go to the
> workingman, especially where he is poor; and in gen-
> eral, go to the poor'. . . .[27]

We have often stressed the popes' insistence that the
apostolate of example is the best way to preach the Good
News to the people. This is especially true where the
poor are concerned. Pius XI stresses this point:

> The most efficacious means of the apostolate among
> the poor and lowly is the priest's example, through
> the practice of all those priestly virtues which We
> have mentioned in Our encyclical, *Ad Catholici Sacer-
> dotii*. Especially needful for the present situation,
> however, is the shining example of a life which is
> humble, poor, and disinterested, in imitation of the
> Divine Master who could say to the world with divine
> simplicity: 'Foxes have earths, birds in the sky have
> nests, but the Son of Man has nowhere that he can
> call his own" (Mt., 8, 20).

> Today a priest who is truly poor and disinterested —
> in the Gospel sense — can work marvels among his
> flock, recalling another St. Vincent de Paul, a Curé of
> Ars, a Cottolengo, a Don Bosco and so many others;
> while an avaricious and selfish priest, as We have also
> noted in the above-mentioned encyclical, even

though he should not plunge with Judas to the depths of treason, will never be more than a hollow 'sounding brass' and a useless 'tinkling cymbal.' Too often, indeed, he will rather be an obstacle than an instrument of grace in the midst of the people.[28]

Through the years, the Franciscans have gone to the poor. Yet there are many who think we can commit ourselves to them yet more fully. Many think we can respond more whole-heartedly to the pleas of the popes by going to those in whom Christ is crucified in our era, the people in the foreign missions, the migrants, the slum dwellers, the sick in mind and body, the hopeless.

Identifying with the Poor

Though each Franciscan may not be able to go to the poor, nevertheless *the order as such must be identified with the poor.* As the Jesuits are popularly identified with education, the Dominicans with theology and philosophy, the Salesians with youth, so must the Franciscans be identified *by the people themselves* as men and women dedicated to the poor. It would be a shame indeed, if the glory of our mission in the Church should fall to any other institute. Should this happen we would have failed Francis, the Church, and God himself. Christ has told us the poor will always be with us. They continue his special presence among us. Where we see the poor we see Christ. What we do for the poor we do for Christ.

The Young Catholic Workers have identified with the poor. We admire their success. The similarity of their ideals and those of Francis is striking. Michael de la Bedoyere in his biography of Msgr. Cardijn (now Cardinal), the founder of the Y.C.W., writes:

He was always putting before those who listened to
him the ideal of consecrating themselves to the working class in order to defend, protect and educate it.
And when he touched on this subject, he at once outlined a lively picture of the Franciscan spirit, for he
believed that the twentieth century would find much
inspiration in the spirit of St. Francis in reaction
against a mounting demand for comfort, pleasure and
pagan living.[29]

The striking resemblance of spirit affords the Franciscan a good opportunity to reassess the spirit of Francis
with reference to modern problems.

The successor to Pius XI was no less direct in his appeal
that the poor be saved for the Church. In fact, Pius XII
was more explicit than *any* modern pope in his counsel
that the Franciscans direct their efforts and energies toward the salvation of the poor. Within a few months after
his election he told the General Chapter of the Franciscans:

In our day when the people are estranged from God,
in large part through a thousand treacherous deceits
and depraved in religious matters no less than in their
social life, they need apostles like St. Francis; apostles
who in every respect are completely loyal to almighty
God; apostles who, by living poor and simple lives,
are out not for their interests but for those of Jesus
Christ and the welfare of souls; apostles who will be
an example to everyone while attracting the poor and
lowly in a special way; apostles filled with exhaust-
less patience toward the defenseless; apostles, finally,
who will be aflame with that unadulterated charity for
everyone which St. Paul describes and extols so ex-

cellently in his canticle (1 Cor., 13).[30]

Ten years later, in 1948, Pius XII was even more explicit. In a letter to Fr. Clement of Milwaukee, Minister General of the Capuchins, the Holy Father wrote:

> The Capuchin Franciscans have from the very beginning made it their special mission to promote and carry on works of the apostolate and charity in favor of the little people, the poor.

> In order that they might accomplish this, the present times demand that they labor with heightened zeal, not only in the churches, for those most in need do not go there, but also by the exercise of their ministry wherever the opportunity presents itself to them as a priest; in the fields, in the shops, factories, hospitals and prisons; in the midst of workers, becoming brothers to brothers to gain all for Christ. Let them mingle their apostolic sweat with that of the workers; let them free their minds from the darkness of error and lead them to the light; let them bestir themselves to soften hearts made hard by hatred and class strife and fill them with divine charity.

> Especially let them understand that the Church is their true mother who is anxious not only for their eternal salvation, but also wants to raise their wretched condition to a more elevated state of life, not by means of fallacious ideologies, riots, and violence, but by justice, equity, and a friendly pacification among the social classes.[31]

Relating with the Negro

Whereas in Europe, among the social classes, the workers may be living in wretched conditions, in the

United States, those who live in the worst conditions are, on the whole, the Indians, the Puerto Ricans, and the Negroes. They should be special concern of the Franciscan today. Because of the present tension, involved in their emergence, we should be relating to the Negro in a special way.

The Catholic Church in the United States is highly regarded by the Negro. In a feature article, using the statistics of Louis Harris, *Newsweek* magazine noted this fact when it said: "Of all whites, Roman Catholic priests, who conduct extensive and little publicized settlement work in Negro communities, are most trusted (by 55 percent of Negroes.)"[32]

The Franciscan order has a wonderful opportunity to seize this chance to reap a bountiful harvest for the kingdom of heaven that Christ's reign might be extended to more hearts. Although we do have priests, brothers, sisters, and tertiaries working among the Negro (and, of course, our cloistered nuns praying for its success), we can have more. The Franciscan order can be proud of the fact that there are many in the Third Order Secular who are very active in this interracial apostolate.

Quietly, effectively, the tertiaries are going about doing good and breaking down prejudices. They are accomplishing their task along the age-old Franciscan plan of action — individual reform leading to social reform. By breaking down individual prejudice, they are doing much to break down local, state, and even national prejudice.

Although the tertiaries are not seeking glory for their work, praise is being heaped upon their efforts. In an article, "A.I.U.: Our Instrument for Interracial Peace," in the *Franciscan Herald and Forum*, the results and the program of the tertiaries are summarized in these words:

Action for Interracial Understanding, our dynamic Third Order program which has been hailed by George K. Hunton, the co-founder of the Catholic interracial movement, as the most important and startling event in the history of the movement, believes that St. Francis has the answers to the tremendous problems that face the relationships of our white and colored fellow human beings. We believe that St. Francis' program for social reform — individual action on the grass roots level, motivated by Christian love — is the fastest and most painless solution to the problem of race relations in America: that is, IF there are enough individuals. . . .[33]

THE THIRD ORDER IN THE AGE OF THE LAYMAN

The Third Order is doing great work in many fields restoring all things in Christ. Here the Franciscan concept of penance resulting in peace for *all* men can best be effected. Here is the instrument to carry on the dialogue of salvation. Although the last few centuries have not been noteworthy, today, however, the tertiaries are making valiant efforts to measure up to the words of Benedict XV in *Sacra Propediem:*

> Above everything else, Francis wanted his tertiaries to be distinguished by a special badge of brotherly love which is keenly solicitous of peace and harmony. Knowing this to be the particular precept of Jesus Christ, containing in itself the fulfillment of the Christian law, he was most anxious to conform the minds of his followers to it. By that very fact he succeeded in rendering the Third Order the greatest boon to human society. . . .

On this immense field of action, to which We as Vicar
of the King of Peace have devoted special care and
thought, We desire to gather the united efforts of all
children of Christian peace and especially these of the
tertiaries, whose influence in restoring peace among
men can be something wonderful, once their number
and their efforts have generally increased.[34]

For years the popes have looked to the Third Order to
be the leaven of society as it was in Francis' day. Pope Leo
XIII looked upon it as his instrument of social reform. "Just
as by the power of God, St. Francis was able to overcome
the evils of the thirteenth century by means of the Third
Order," he wrote, "so now I am firmly convinced that in
our own age the Third Order is the most efficacious remedy to cure the present evils and to bring back the world
to the true and solid practice of the Gospel."[35] In his
apostolic letter, *La Principale Gloria*, Pope Pius X indicated that he wanted the Third Order to be an instrument
in fulfilling his motto of restoring all things in Christ.[36]
Thus, decades ago these popes realized the value of the layman in reforming society.

The Layman and World-Renewal

Today we live in the *age* of the layman. No longer will
the people of the world be saved by the priests alone. The
people of the world will also be saved by their own. This
is probably why Pope Paul said:

The layman should arrive at a knowledge of this fact
which is true not only by reason of the need for
lengthening the arms of the priest which do not reach
everywhere, but also because they are not sufficient in
themselves for all his labors.[37]

If the layman must realize this, so should the priest. The Second Vatican Council has shown that laymen will be the priests' best instruments in revitalizing society. The Third Order can also be the best instrument of the First Order. As Pope John said to the tertiaries of Italy: "An apostolate of this kind can be considered a great help to the priesthood. It can be one of the most lively and laudable forces in winning for us the blessings of God."[38]

Franciscans have a wonderful instrument in the Third Order, and the Third Order has a wonderful means to effect this revitalization of society through the Franciscan spirit. In this age of *aggiornamento*, the words of Pope Pius XII take on special meaning:

> It may well be said that whenever the Church called her children together for any work of profound internal renewal, she found the tertiaries ready to cooperate in ensuring the success of the common effort.[39]

The Third Order was founded to effect just such a reformation. Leo XIII once wrote:

> Domestic peace and public tranquility, integrity of life and courtesy, the right use and management of property — which are the best foundation of civilization and security — spring from the Third Order of St. Francis as from their root.[40]

Likewise, Pope Pius X wrote:

> Thus was the Third Order established; and it proved beneficial to Church and State, as long as it clung religiously to its original ideal of penance. There can be no doubt, therefore, that it will produce similar fruit if it will but retain the ideal to the same extent.[41]

Again Pope Benedict wrote in a similar vein:

> We believe that the spirit of the Third Order, thoroughly redolent of Gospel wisdom, will do very much to reform public and private morals, if only it is made to flourish as it did in the time of Francis when he preached the Kingdom of God everywhere by word and deed.[42]

Effectiveness of the Third Order

Despite the commendations of the popes, some people still insist the Third Order is not fully qualified to carry out the reform the popes expect of it. They may single out an organization like Y.C.W. for special support, little realizing how much the principles of St. Francis form the basis of its program. "There are so many things which the world thinks impossible," Cardinal Cardijn wrote:

> The force of the good, properly organized, has yet to give the results that one may justifiably expect. I foresee a kind of professional 'third order,' preached and organized by new *poverellos* of Assisi. We need more boldness to make the world happy. We must allow ourselves to be overcome by that holy wrath which sometimes seized our Savior before the abuses and hypocrisies of his contemporaries.[43]

Even though other groups are doing wonderful work in the Church, we must not neglect the special task given us by the Church. If the Third Order has failed, then the First Order has failed. The popes have given the Third Order to the First Order to be its special reforming agent in society. Summing up this whole problem with a very cogent answer, Pope Pius XII said:

While no one harbors any doubts about the importance of the Franciscan Third Order in the modern world, still worthy of note are the anxieties which the most zealous Franciscans feel about the effective vitality of the Third Order both in Italy and in other countries: there are some who fear that the Third Order today does not give the hosts of saints and apostles that it once provided for the complete service of the Church.

The reasons for such a phenomenon may perhaps be sought — among other things — in a lesser efficacy of the Franciscan spirit in not a few tertiaries, and at times in some directors. That is to say, some complain that matters frequently remain too much in the field of theory, when in reality, it is not sufficient to know the life of the Holy Patriarch and to tell it to others in order to be sure of forming oneself and especially others according to the Franciscan outlook and method.[44]

What Pope Pius XII is telling us is this: too often we have been content with talking about Francis and his reform of penance without putting his ideal into practice.

It is the God-given task of the members of the Franciscan family, especially the directors and members of the Third Order to devise new and practical means enabling the Third Order to be effective. Principles used in other groups can be increased and made meaningful. Ways in which secular societies and activities can be given Christian leadership (which is one of the main ways society will be reformed) should be investigated diligently.

The Third Order has been revitalized by the modern popes, especially by Pope Leo XIII with the new Rule and by Pope Pius XII with the new Constitutions to make it fit the needs of the times with a way of perfection suitable to modern living and adaptable to modern expressions of spiritual formation and apostolic activities.

What should be done to remedy any false impressions we might have about the value of the Third Order is, first of all, to develop a greater realization of its inherent potential for good. The words of Pope Pius XI to the bishops of the entire world are no less applicable to the followers of St. Francis:

> The earnest wishes, which our predecessors Leo XIII, in the encyclical *Auspicato,* and Benedict XV, in *Sacra Propediem,* signified to the bishops of the whole Catholic world, We also hope to see brought about with the pastoral cooperation of all of you; namely, that you will promote the Third Order of St. Francis in every way, by teaching your flock either personally or through competent preachers what is the purpose of this order of men and women in the world; how highly it is to be esteemed; how easily it is to enter the order and observe its holy rule; what a wealth of indulgences and privileges the tertiaries enjoy and what a blessing the Third Order is to the individual and the community. Urge those who have not yet entered this distinguished militia to do so this year and let those who are too young to join become Cordbearers of St. Francis so that even the children may grow accustomed to this way of life.[45]

Secondly, let us be true to our vocation. "We cannot understand how it is," Pope Pius XI wrote to Leonard Bello, the Minister General of the Friars Minor, that after the repeated summons of the late popes, Our venerable predecessors, and of Ourselves, both in encyclicals and in personal audiences, there are still persons who not only neglect the Third Order but actually antagonize it. Their responsibility is great for thus depriving souls of an exceptional blessing.[46]

In a similar manner the ministers general themselves wrote, using the strong words:

Whoever failed to feel this duty in conscience for the life and promotion of the Third Order, would be failing in his own vocation, would be a traitor to the work of our Seraphic Father and would be defrauding souls of their welfare.[47]

Finally, it is a matter of updating our techniques to make the Third Order more appealing to the modern, active Catholic.

The Third Order is our means to bring the world to Christ through penance. The popes have made it so. It is an effective way to lead souls on a way of perfection. By baptism a Christian is called to perfection. He has a vocation to take up Christ's cross, to follow him, to imitate him, to live on in his love. "The end or goal of the Christian life, in all its fulness," Pope John has stated, "is that everyone, even though remaining in the lay state, strive nevertheless after Christian perfection."[48] "In the Third Order of St. Francis," he also said, "one has a truly solid foundation and the blessed opportunity to make progress in the spiritual life."[49]

The Third Order helps the laity lead lives reflecting the Gospel counsels and helps them lead others to follow the Gospel teachings.

The promotion of the Third Order is the obligation of the whole Franciscan family. The tertiaries themselves must live their lives to the fullest perfection if they are to bear fruit in the kingdom of Christ. Their vocation in the Church is to live the life of penance in response to God's love for all men and to be a leaven in society that others will turn to God. As Pope Benedict XV wrote:

> It is for them to study the life of their Father; to consider his close and evident similarity to Jesus Christ, especially in the way he fled the comforts of the world and embraced suffering by which he merited for himself both the name of the Poverello and the reception in his body of the wounds of the Crucified. It is for them to show that they have not degenerated from his ideal, by embracing poverty at least in the spirit, by mortifying themselves, and by carrying their crosses.

> It is the special duty of our tertiary sisters to be in their appearance and their whole manner of life, an object lesson of holy modesty to other young girls and women. Let them be assured that they can render no better service to the Church or State than by paving the way for the reformation of corrupt morals. And when the members of the order have organized various methods of benevolence to help the needy in their many wants, they will, like true brothers, surely not be guilty of withholding the works of their charity from those who are in need of far greater than earthly goods.

> Here We are reminded of the words of St. Peter, calling the Christians to be an example to the nations of a

holy life, that 'although they may in the usual way
slander you as evil-doers yet when disasters come,
they may glorify God when they see how well you
conduct yourselves' (1 Pet. 2, 12). In a like manner, so
should our Franciscan tertiaries, by purity of faith,
by innocence of life, and by cheerful zeal diffuse the
good odor of Christ far and wide and be to the brethren who have gone astray both a reminder and an in-
vitation to come to a sense of their duties. This the
Church asks; this she expects of them.[50]

This the Church asks; this the Church expects of all
of us. Today the need for penance is more urgent than ever.
Each of us is to be a reminder to the world to turn to Christ.
Each of us, by our lives, is to become the conscience of
Christianity, gently admonishing the world to turn its heart
to God.

Building up the Body of Christ

This is essential for every Christian, for every Franciscan. God has loved the world so much that he has given
it his Christ to show it how to live. Christ has loved us so
much that he has died for us that we might live in him.
In return, then, our lives must be lived through him in a
return of love to our heavenly Father and so must the
lives of all the People of God.

As part of the universal "we" of humanity redeemed
by Christ, we are responsible for its salvation. All people
must become the People of God, all must become the *ana-*
wim of the Father of Lights. We must, as members of the
Church, Pope Paul says, "be always ready to carry on
the dialogue with all men of good will. . . . There is no one
who can be a stranger to its heart, no one in whom its
ministry has no interest."[51]

By living our Franciscan vocation as the popes, the voices of Christ in our age, would have us do, we will best achieve our mission in the Church — which, like the vocation of the Church itself, is to serve, to be of service to the world. "To work then, you, too, beloved children!" Pius XII has said to us in his address to the tertiaries:

> Jesus tells you so through the mouth of his Vicar, however unworthy. Let all join forces together, bringing aid to the world. Support the Church, in whose members, though error and evil are not absent sad to say, there is nevertheless still so much heroism, so much holiness.[52]

The Third Order way is the Christian way. It is our way to make the world truly Catholic. This is why Pope Pius XI made the bold statement which should be our conviction as well:

> To those who are not yet tertiaries We would say: Become tertiaries! For while it may be true that this is not strictly necessary, it is necessary in so far as the spirit of the Third Order is the spirit not only of St. Francis but of Jesus Christ as well, and that spirit all of us must have![53]

It is our duty, then, "to make of the Third Order a school of Christian perfection of the genuine Franciscan spirit and of the fearless and prompt action for the building up of the Body of Christ."[54] The world is ours to give to Christ. Christ lives in us that he might draw the world to himself to sanctify it anew. Today more than ever before, the world is in need of our Franciscan *Weltanschauung,* of our Franciscan vision of life.

CONCLUSION

The words of Pope Pius XII to the tertiaries should be
a rallying call for every son and daughter of St. Francis.
They should be a constant challenge to every Franciscan
who wants to live in union with the Church's spirit and
life as the popes have outlined. Pius XII declared:

> Society has an urgent need of this spirit, not only for
> its peace, happiness, and prosperity, but in a way, for
> its very existence. It is for you, sons and daughters
> of St. Francis . . . to make that spirit sparkle and radi-
> ate.[55]

"It is your duty, beloved children, to know it thoroughly,
to love it with enthusiasm and above all, to live it with
the perfection that your state in life allows."[56]

The popes, as Vicars of Christ on earth, have given us
an outline of our vocation to relive Christ and Francis in
our age. Our role in the Church today is to witness to what
Francis was for the Church in his day: another Christ.
Our vocation is to put on the mind of Francis, as he put
on the mind of Christ, being totally subservient at the
feet of the Holy Roman Church. This means to find in the
words of the popes the present will of Christ for us. This
means being driven on by the Spirit of Christ by living
in the life of the Church, the liturgy. This means living
the life in a spirit of penance in a total response and commitment to God's love for us in Christ by drawing all men
to him and his Church as the popes so earnestly desire.
As members of Christ and members of the Seraphic Family, we have been committed to carry on the dialogue of
salvation which the Church is carrying on with the modern
world. Through our lives of penance we will help convert

the world by truly loving it.

Our vocation in the Church is to become afire with the love of God, living intense interior lives. Poverty, charity, and humility should permeate our lives so we can spread this same spirit to all men, especially to the little ones, the poor who are pilgrimaging in this world, seeking that peace which Christ came to give.

If we fulfill these wishes of the popes for us, we will bear fruit in the Church of Christ. We will bring the People of God to share more fully in his kingdom on earth. By living the Franciscan spirit and by spreading it to others, we will be the modern St. Francis which the world needs. Like Francis, each one of us will be able to enkindle the world with a seraphic kind of love, leading it to the Heart of God. We have been called in the dialogue of salvation to make a response. We have been given a vocation. We must bear witness to the reality of the Christian message in our day.

This, in the mind of the popes, is what it means to be a follower of Francis today. This is what it means to truly fulfill that rule which we have promised the Lord to obey. As Pope John XXIII said on the seven hundred and fiftieth anniversary of the approval of our rule:

> Beloved brothers in St. Francis: to Ourselves, to you, and to everyone. We repeat the great admonition which comes to us from heaven: this is the great *Rule* we honor; this is the path which leads to life; this is the way which leads to blessing and glory. *Alleluia. Alleluia.*[57]

Notes

Preface

1. *LTC,* n. 48 (de Robeck, p. 86).
2. 1 Cel., n. 33 (Hermann, p. 19); cf. *LTC,* n. 49.
3. John XXIII, *Questi Primi Mesi,* April 16, 1959, *AAS* 51 (1959), pp. 307-308; cf. *TPS* 6, 4 (1959-1960), pp. 350-351.
4. As Pope John XXIII stated to the members of the First International Congress on Vocations to the States of Perfection (*L'Incontro Odierno,* December 17, 1961, *AAS* 54 [1962], p. 35; cf. *Today's Vocation Crisis,* trans. and ed. Godfrey Poage C.P. and Germain Lievin C.SS.R. [Westminster, Maryland: The Newman Press, 1962], p. 6): "At times the contemplative life is misunderstood. Some fail to comprehend the fact that in all its perfection, by its prayers and reparation, it is essentially directed towards the apostolate. Thus Our Predecessor, Pope Pius XI, explained: 'Much more is contributed to the growth and development of the Church by contemplative groups than by those who perform the actual labors, for it is they who call down from heaven the vivifying graces to irrigate the upturned fields of the other evangelical workers' (*Umbratilem,* July 8, 1924, *AAS* 16 [1924], p. 389)."
5. Cf. especially Pius XII, *Sponsa Christi,* November 21, 1950, *AAS* 43 (1951), pp. 12 ff; cf. Courtois, pp. 159 ff. and Pius XII, *Cedant Voluntries,* July 20, 27, and August 3, 1958, *AAS* 50 (1958), pp. 579 ff; cf. *TPS* 5, 1 (1958-1959), pp. 75 ff.
6. Cf. Paul VI, *Ecclesiam Suam,* August 6, 1964, *AAS* 56 (1964); NCWC, *ad passim.*
7. *LTC,* n. 46 (de Robeck, p. 85; *Words,* pp. 55-56).
8. "Thus did Francis make himself the 'vir Ecclesiae,' the vassal

of the Lord Pope, ready to fulfill his commands and undertake his mandates. This carries over into our present rule as 'Brother Francis promises obedience and reverence to the Lord Pope Honorius and to his lawful successors, and to the Roman Church.' Let us note that this was the first time in the history of the Church that an order as a whole had so closely bound itself to the pope and put itself so completely under him in all things." Cajetan Esser O.F.M., "'Melius Catholice Observemus,'" in The Marrow of the Gospel, trans. and ed. Ignatius Brady O.F.M. (Chicago: Franciscan Herald Press, 1958), p. 113. Words, p. 211.

Chapter One
"AT THE FEET OF THE SAME HOLY CHURCH"

1. Pius XI, Rite Expiatis, April 30, 1926, AAS 18 (1926), p. 172; cf. RHS, p. 62.

2. John XXIII, Questi Primi Mesi, April 16, 1959, AAS 51 (1959), p. 311; cf. TPS 6, 4 (1959-1960), p. 354.

3. John Cogley, "Another Saint Francis?," The Commonweal 58, 14 (June 28, 1963), pp. 367-369.

4. According to Pope Pius XII, writing on the seventh centenary of the death of St. Clare (Proximo Mense, May 25, 1953, OR 93, 113, (June 11, 1953), p. 1; cf. FHF 32, 9, p. 259): "While we reflect again on the life of this holy citizen of heaven and reverently recall what she did under the influence of divine grace and what has been done by the community she founded as well as by those which have sprung from it . . . we do not hesitate to declare that the Church as well as civil society owe very much to this holy virgin."

5. Third Rule, 12 (Words, p. 294).

6. Leo XIII, Au Milieu, December 23, 1900, Acta Leonis 20 (1901), p. 340; ASS 33 (1900-1901), p. 356.

7. Leo XIII, Testem Benevolentiae, January 22, 1899, Acta Leonis 19 (1900), p. 16; ASS 31 (1898-1899), p. 477.

8. 2 Cel., n. 24 (Hermann, p. 96; Words, pp. 213-214).

9. The Rule and General Constitutions of Friars Minor, Constitutions, n. 10 (New Jersey: St. Anthony Guild Press, 1936), p. 3.

10. John XXIII, Questi Primi Mesi, AAS, p. 310; cf. TPS, p. 353.

11. Pius XI, *Rite Expiatis, AAS*, p. 163; cf. *RHS*, p. 53.

12. Paul VI, *Ecclesiam Suam*, August 6, 1964, *AAS* 56 (1964) p. 624; cf. NCWC, p. 13.

13. Paul VI, *E Motivo*, September 8, 1964, *OR* 104, 208, (September 9, 1964), p. 1.

14. In regard to the value of encyclicals in particular, Pope Pius XII (*Humani Generis*, August 12, 1950, *AAS* 42 (1950), p. 568; cf. NCWC, n. 20, p. 10) makes it clear that: "It cannot be thought that what is treated in the encyclical letters does not of itself demand consent, because in writing such letters the popes do not exercise the supreme power of their teaching authority. In reality, these matters are taught with the ordinary teaching authority, about which the saying is true, 'Whoever is listening to you is listening to me' (Lk. 10, 16). Generally, what is treated and inculcated in encyclical letters does already appertain to Catholic doctrine for other reasons."

15. Pius XII, *Vos Omnes*, September 10, 1957, *AAS* 49 (1957), p. 807; cf. *TPS* 4, 4 (1957-1958), p. 448.

16. Karl Rahner S.J., *The Christian Commitment*, trans. Cecily Hastings (New York: Sheed and Ward, 1963), p. 141.

17. *Ibid.*

18. *Ibid.*

19. Third Rule, 1 (*Words*, p. 285).

20. *Constitutions of the Order of Friars Minor Conventual* n. 26, (Province of Our Lady of Consolation, private printing, 1945), pp. 26-27.

21. *Rule and Constitutions, Franciscan Third Order*, Constitutions, n. 95 (Chicago: Franciscan Herald Press, 1959), p. 47.

22. John XXIII, *Cum Natalicia*, April 4, 1959, *AAS* 51 (1959), p. 298; cf. *FHF* 38, 7 (1959), p. 220.

23. Paul VI, *E Motivo, OR*, p. 1.

24. Letter to All the Faithful (*Words,* p. 188).

25. Letter to All the Custodes (*Words*, p. 164).

26. Pius XII, *Mediator Dei*, November 20, 1947, *AAS* 39 (1947), p. 532; cf. NCWC, n. 26, p. 13.

27. John XXIII, *Al Saluto Scambiato*, November 23, 1958, *OR* 98, 274 (November 24-25, 1958), pp. 1-2; cf. *TPS* 5, 3 (1958-1959), pp. 283-286.

28. Giovanni Battista Montini, to the Liturgical Study Week at

Vecenza, quoted in H. Schutte, *Um die Wiedervereinigung im Glauben* 2nd. ed. (Essen, 1959), p. 148. In regard to the value of the Pope's words before his elevation to the papacy, Augustin Cardinal Bea writes ("Forward," in Walsh, p. xvi): "Naturally, in considering the declarations of the pope in this broader light the reader must be careful to bear in mind, so to speak, the 'hierarchy' existing between the various declarations reproduced in the book. The declarations of the pope are indeed the determining ones, whereas those made prior to the pontificate are subsidiary, an aid towards the fuller understanding of the former and not to be used for the purpose of interpreting in any other than their true sense the acts and words of the Pontiff."

29. Cajetan Esser O.F.M. and Engelbert Grau O.F.M., *Love's Reply*, trans. Ignatius Brady O.F.M. (Chicago: Franciscan Herald Press, 1963), p. 97.

30. Father James O.S.F.C., *The Franciscans* (New York: The Macmillan Company, 1930), pp. 23-24.

Chapter Two

THE LIFE OF PENANCE IN THE CHURCH

1. John XXIII, *Cum Natalicia*, April 4, 1959, AAS 51 (1959), pp. 297-298; cf. FHF 38, 7 (1959), p. 220.

2. Leo XIII, *Auspicato*, September 17, 1882, Acta Leonis 3 (1884), pp. 144-145; ASS 15 (1882), p. 146; cf. RHS, pp. 12-13.

3. Paul VI, *Ecclesiam Suam*, August 6, 1964, AAS 56 (1964), p. 642; cf. NCWC, p. 27.

4. The Letter to the Christians at Ephesus, 2, 14.

5. Joel 2, 12-13.

6. John XXIII, *Paenitentiam Agere*, July 1, 1962, AAS 54 (1962), p. 482; cf. TPS 8, 2 (1961-1962), p. 112.

7. S. Laurentii a Brundusio, *Opera Omnia*, 5, Quadragesimale Secundum, pars 3 (Patavii: Officina Typographica Seminarii, 1940), p. 235.

8. *Ibid.*, p. 238.

9. Nevin Crosby O.F.M.Cap., "Penance-Metanoia in the Sacred Scriptures," (unpublished paper, Marathon, Wisconsin, 1963), pp. 1-2. I would like to thank Father Nevin for much of the back-

ground information used in the first few pages of this chapter.

10. Paul VI, *Ecclesiam Suam*, AAS, p. 642; cf. NCWC, p. 27.

11. Micah 2, 12-13; 4, 6-7.

12. Jer. 31, 31-34.

13. Mt. 3, 1-2.

14. John XXIII, *Paenitentiam Agere*, AAS, p. 483; cf. *TPS*, pp. 112-113. The footnotation in AAS for the Scriptural reference does not agree with the standard reference.

15. Mk. 1,14-15.

16. Lk. 4,16-21.

17. Mt. 18,1-4.

18. John XXIII, *Paenitentiam Agere*, AAS, p. 483; cf. *TPS*, p. 113.

19. Jer. 24, 7.

20. Mt. 11,29.

21. Mk. 10,45.

22. Leo XIII, *Auspicato*, Acta Leonis 3 (1884), p. 145; ASS, pp. 146-147; cf. *RHS*, p. 13. In the words of Celano (1 Cel. n. 89 [Hermann, p. 46]), "when the teachings of the Gospel, not indeed in every respect, but taken generally, had everywhere failed to be put into practice, this man was sent by God to bear *witness to the truth* throughout the whole world in accordance with the example of the Apostles. And thus it came to pass that his teaching showed that the wisdom of *this world* is most evidently *turned to foolishness,* and within a short period of time brought it, under the guidance of Christ, to the true wisdom of God *by the foolishness* of his *preaching.* for in this *last time* this new evangelist, like one of the rivers that flowed out of paradise, diffused the waters of the Gospel over the whole world by his tender watering, and preached by his deeds the way of the Son of God and the doctrine of truth. Accordingly, in him and through him there arose throughout the world an unlooked for happiness and holy newness, and a shoot of the ancient religion suddenly brought a great renewal to those who had grown calloused and to the very old. A new spirit was born in the hearts of the elect, and a saving unction was poured out in their midst, when the servant of the holy man of Christ, like one of the lights of the heavens, shone brilliantly with a new rite and with new signs."

23. Pius XII, *Generalis Capituli,* June 5, 1939, *Discoursi e Radiomessaggi di Sua Santita Piu XII,* I (Milano: Societa Editrice "Vita

e Pensiero," 1941), p. 160; cf. *The Third Order Forum* 18, 9 (1939), pp. 207-208.

24. John XXIII, *Cum Natalicia, AAS,* p. 298; cf. *FHF,* p. 220.

25. Paul VI, *Ecclesiam Suam, AAS,* p. 642; cf. NCWC, p. 27.

26. Page of Praises for Brother Leo (*Words,* pp. 23-24).

27. Pius XII, *Nel Darvi,* July 1, 1956, *AAS* 48 (1956), p. 576; cf. *RHS,* p. 74.

28. *Ibid.*

29. Paul VI, to Augustine Sepinski O.F.M. and the General Definitorium O.F.M., *FHF* 44, 4 (1964), p. 103.

30. First Rule, 23 (*Words,* pp. 282-283).

31. John XXIII, *Paenitentiam Agere, AAS,* p. 481; cf. *TPS,* p. 111.

32. Paul VI, *Ecclesiam Suam, AAS,* p. 643; cf. NCWC, p. 27.

33. Mk. 3,31-35.

34. Letter to All the Faithful (*Words,* p. 190).

35. Cajetan Esser O.F.M. and Engelbert Grau O.F.M., *Love's Reply,* trans. Ignatius Brady O.F.M. (Chicago: Franciscan Herald Press, 1963), p. 94. (cf. ft. 29, ch. 1).

36. Pius XI, *Caritate Christi Compulsi,* May 3, 1932, *AAS* 24 (1932), p. 191; cf. Husslein, p. 274.

37. Paul VI, *Ecclesiam Suam, AAS,* p. 639; NCWC, p. 25.

38. Leon Joseph Cardinal Suenens, *The Nun in the World,* trans. Geoffrey Stevens (Westminster, Maryland: The Newman Press, 1962), pp. 24-25.

39. Cf. Chapter One.

40. Pius XII, *Nel Darvi, AAS,* p. 576; cf. *RHS,* p. 74.

41. Paul VI, Homily on the Feast of St. Francis, October 4, 1964, *OR* 104, 231 (October 5-6, 1964), p. 1

42. Pius XI, *Rite Expiatis,* April 30, 1926, *AAS* 18 (1926), p. 154; cf. *RHS,* p. 44.

43. In his 1964 Christmas address (*La Ricorrenza,* December 22, 1964, *OR* 104, 298 (December 24, 1964), p. 1), Pope Paul VI stressed that one of the main obstacles to brotherhood is selfishness in the world. Both selfishness and lack of love (which are basically the same) result from a lack of true knowledge about something. This is probably why Pope John XXIII (*Ad Petri Cathedram,* June 29, 1959, AAS 51 (1959), p. 498; cf. TPS 5, 4 (1958-1959), p. 360) wrote that "all the evils" in the world have as their root ignorance.

44. Benedict XV, *Sacra Propediem*, January 6, 1921, *AAS* 13 (1921), p. 36; cf. *RHS*, pp. 34-35.
45. John XXIII, *La Nostra Prima*, June 5, 1960, *AAS* 52 (1960), p. 520; cf. *TPS* 6, 3 (1959-1960), p. 234.
46. Giovanni Battista Montini, radio message for the mission of Milan, 1957, cf. Walsh, p. 3.
47. Giovanni Battista Montini, to the Second World Lay Apostolic Congress, October 7, 1957, *OR* 97, 235 (October 10, 1957), p. 2; cf. Walsh, p. 21.

Chapter Three
THE FIRE WITHIN

1. Paul VI, *Ecclesiam Suam*, August 6, 1964, *AAS* 56 (1964), p. 637; cf. NCWC, p. 23.
2. Paul VI, to Augustine Sepinski O.F.M. and the General Definitorium O.F.M., *FHF* 44, 4 (1964), p. 102.
3. Testament (*Words*, p. 245).
4. Paul VI, *op. cit.*, p. 103.
5. Testament of St. Clare, 2, *The Legend and Writings of Saint Clare of Assisi* (St. Bonaventure, New York: The Franciscan Institute, 1953), p. 82.
6. *Mirror of Perfection*, 76 (*Words*, p. 109; cf. 2 Cel., n. 208 [Hermann, p. 199]).
7. Benedict XV, *Sacra Propediem*, January 6, 1921, *AAS* 13 (1921), p. 40; cf. *RHS*, p. 38.
8. Pius XII, *Mystici Corporis*, May 29, 1943, *AAS* 35 (1943), pp. 214-215; cf. NCWC, n. 47, pp. 18-19.
9. In a fine passage (which has been condensed here), Hans Urs von Balthasar shows, in the historical context, what can happen in the Mystical Body when the personification of a cell (for us, St. Francis) is viewed, in practice, as separated from its relation to the whole Body: "The many possibilities contained in the Word, temporarily suppressed by the fearful and traditionalistic early Middle Ages, which overthrew multiplicity in favor of abstract unity, finally blossomed in the twelfth century. At this time people in various states of life — hierarchy, regular clergy, secular clergy,

and laity — became aware of their qualitative differences and began to try to determine their special place in the Church. It was
only when Francis and Dominic appeared beside Benedict that the
mysterious force of the founder-personality became visible; to them
it was granted to forge a religious 'family,' and this more deeply
than in a merely psychological way. This was probably the first
instance of what we call 'special spirituality.' This was a great gift
indeed! But it also brought a great danger of giving a worldly interpretation to the charism of the founder, and of looking only
at the image of the saint instead of keeping one's eyes fixed on
Christ. This did happen to the Franciscan Spirituals and is a constant threat to all who are not sufficiently forearmed.

"The different spiritualities do not arise solely because of the
creature-conditioned perspective of the truth, nor because of the
historical and personal circumstances of the subject, nor because
of the individualization involved in transforming objective doctrine into subjective assimilation and experience. All these elements play a part, but they are subordinate to God's free allotment
of his gifts and charisms. 'Each man is given his gift by the Spirit
that he may use it for the common good. . . . Behind all these
gifts is the operation of the same Spirit, who distributes to each
individual man, as he wills.' (1 Cor., 12:4,11, cf. Eph., 4:11-13)
The essence of the different spiritualities is not determined, therefore, by the person of the recipient, but by the mandate from on
high, which can never be reckoned and delimited in an empirico-
psychological way, because its source is the free will of God and
its end is to fill out the structure of the Mystical Body." Hans Urs
von Balthasar, "*Spiritualitat*," *Geist und Leben* 31, 5 (1958), pp.
345-346. *Theology Digest* (10, 4 [1962], pp. 191-192) carries a
condensation of this article. However, on page 192 read "Franciscan Spirituals" for "Franciscan mystics."

10. Salute to the Virtues (*Words*, p. 73).
11. Pius XI, *Rite Expiatis*, April 30, 1926, *AAS* 18 (1926), p. 166;
cf. *RHS*, p. 56.
12. Cajetan Esser O.F.M., *Repair My House*, trans. Michael D.
Meilach O.F.M. (Chicago: Franciscan Herald Press, 1963), p. 115.
13. Pius XII, *Se l' Umanita*, September 20, 1945, *COFMConv.*,
42 (1945), p. 241; cf. *RHS*, pp. 66-67.

14. Pius XII, *Nel Darvi,* July 1, 1956, *AAS* 48 (1956), p. 576; cf. *RHS,* p. 75.

15. Paul VI, to Augustine Sepinski O.F.M. and the General Definitorium O.F.M., *FHF* 44, 4 (1964), p. 103.

16. Pius XI, *Caritate Christi Compulsi,* May 3, 1932, *AAS* 24 (1932), p. 191; cf. Husslein, p. 274.

17. In *Questi Primi Mesi,* April 16, 1959, *AAS* 51 (1959), pp. 309 ff., Pope John XXIII says that the three virtues characteristic of the Franciscan Family are poverty, obedience (to Rome) and charity, especially in its relation to the mission spirit. We have seen in Chapter One that obedience to the popes is the very foundation of the Franciscan Spirit. Charity viewed as the spreading of the love of God to all nations will be treated in Chapters Four and Six. The words of the popes, taken *in toto,* show that the three characteristics of the *interior* spirit are those developed in this chapter, namely, poverty, charity and humility.

18. Paul VI, Homily on the Feast of St. Francis, October 4, 1964, OR 104, 231 (October 5-6, 1964), p. 1.

19. *Leg. Maj.* 8, c. 7, n. 1, p. 523.

20. Pius XI, *Rite Expiatis, AAS,* pp. 158-159; cf. *RHS,* pp. 48-49.

21. *Ibid.,* p. 160; cf. *RHS,* p. 50.

22. Paul VI, *Magno Gaudio Affecti,* May 23, 1964, *AAS* 56 (1964), p. 567; cf. *TPS* 9, 4 (1963-1964), p. 398.

23. Pius XI, *Rite Expiatis, AAS,* p. 165; cf. RHS, p. 55.

24. *Constitutions of the Capuchin Friars Minor of St. Francis,* n. 97 (Province of St. Joseph of the Capuchin Order, Detroit, 1945), p. 49.

25. John XXIII, *Due Nomi Luminosi,* October 4, 1962, *AAS* 54 (1962), pp. 728-729; cf. *FHF* 42, 2 (1963), pp. 55-56.

26. *LTC,* n. 9 (*Words,* p. 117).

27. Paul VI, to Augustine Sepinski O.F.M. and the General Definitorium O.F.M., *FHF* 44, 4 (1964), p. 103.

28. Pius XII, *Nel Darvi, AAS,* p. 577; cf. *RHS,* p. 75.

29. Pius XI, *Rite Expiatis, AAS,* p. 165; cf. *RHS,* p. 55.

30. Leo XIII, *Auspicato,* September 17, 1882, *Acta Leonis* 3 (1884), p. 147; *ASS* 15 (1882), p. 148; cf. *RHS,* p. 14.

31. *Ibid., Acta Leonis,* pp. 147-148; *ASS,* p. 148; cf. *RHS,* pp. 14-15.

32. *Words*, p. 93.

33. Lk. 3, 7-14.

34. Pius XII, *Se l' Umanita*, COFMConv., p. 241; cf. *RHS*, pp. 66-67.

35. 2 Cel., n. 140 (Hermann, p. 157).

36. *Ibid.*, n. 148 (p. 162)

37. Pius XI, *Rite Expiatis*, AAS, pp. 160-161; cf. *RHS*. pp. 50-51.

38. *Ibid.*, AAS, p. 161; cf. *RHS*, p. 51.

39. *Ibid.*, AAS, pp. 161-162; cf. *RHS*, pp. 51-52.

Chapter Four

CASTING THE FIRE

1. Pius XI, *Rite Expiatis*, April 30, 1926, AAS 18 (1926), p. 162; cf. *RHS*, p. 52.

2. *LTC*, n. 36 (de Robeck, p. 73).

3. Pius XI, *Rite Expiatis*, AAS, p. 167; cf. *RHS*, p. 57.

4. 2 Cel., n. 155 (Hermann, p. 164).

5. Leo XIII, *Auspicato*, September 17, 1882, *Acta Leonis* 3 (1884), pp. 149-150; ASS 15 (1882), p. 149; cf. *RHS*, p. 16.

6. Pius XII, *Ammirevole Spettacolo*, May 5, 1940, AAS 32 (1940), p. 186.

7. Pius XI, *Rite Expiatis*, AAS, p. 169; cf. *RHS*, p. 59.

8. *Ibid.*, AAS, pp. 158-159; cf. *RHS*, pp. 46-49.

9. Pius XII, *Ammirevole Spettacolo*, AAS, p. 185.

10. 1 Cel., n. 76 (Hermann, p. 38; *Words*, p. 77).

11. Leo XIII, *Auspicato*, *Acta Leonis*, p. 150; ASS, p. 149; cf. *RHS*, p. 16.

12. Pius XII, *Nel Darvi*, July 1, 1956, AAS 48 (1956), p. 575; cf. *RHS*, p. 73.

13. Pius X, St., to the tertiaries of Florence, August 15, 1913, Peruffo, p. 289.

14. Pius X, St., to the tertiaries of Lazio, April 28, 1912, Peruffo, p. 279.

15. Leo XIII, *Humanum Genus*, April 20, 1884, *Acta Leonis* 4 (1885), p. 66; ASS 16 (1883), pp. 430-431; cf. William J. Whalen, *Christianity and American Freemasonry*, "Appendix" (Milwaukee, The Bruce Publishing Company, 1958), p. 182.

16. Pius XI, *Non e Piccolo*, February 26, 1923, *AOFM* 42-43 (1923-1924), p. 122; cf. *RHS*, p. 41.

17. Leo XIII, *Auspicato, Acta Leonis*, pp. 152-153; *ASS*, p. 151; cf. *RHS*, pp. 18-19.

18. Paul VI, Homily on the Feast of St. Francis, October 4, 1964, *OR*, 104, 231 (October 5-6, 1964), p. 1.

19. Pius XII, *Ammirevole Spettacolo, AAS*, p. 186.

20. John XXIII, to the tertiaries of Italy, July 2, 1961, *OR* 101, 153 (July 5, 1961), p. 1.

21. *Chicago Tribune*, June 22, 1963, p. 8.

22. Pius XII, *Se l'Umanita*, September 20, 1945, *COFMConv.* 42 (1945), p. 243; cf. *RHS*, p. 70.

23. Pius XII, *Generalis Capituli*, June 5, 1939, *Discorsi e Radiomessaggi di Sua Santita Pio XII* (Milano: Societa Editrice "Vita e Pensiero," 1941), pp. 159-160; cf. *The Third Order Forum* 18, 9 (1939), pp. 207-208.

Chapter Five

REKINDLING THE SPIRIT

1. Since Pope Pius XI wrote these words, the secular institutes have increased in importance. This includes the Franciscan-based secular institutes, especially the Missionaries of the Kingship of Christ which numbers several thousand members.

2. Pius XI, *Rite Expiatis*, April 30, 1926, *AAS* 18 (1926), p. 173; cf. *RHS*, p. 63.

3. Paul VI, to Augustine Sepinski O.F.M. and the General Definitorium O.F.M., *FHF* 44, 4 (1964), p. 103.

4. John XXIII, *Cum Natalicia*, April 4, 1959, *AAS* 51 (1959), p. *FHF* 38, 7 (1959), p. 221.

5. Leon Joseph Cardinal Suenens, *The Nun in the World*, trans. Geoffrey Stevens (Westminster, Maryland: The Newman Press, 1962), pp. 34-35. That, by the grace of God, the Franciscan order will always have a place in the Church can be found in the narration of a revelation given Francis concerning the state of the order and the fact that the order would never fail is recorded in 2 Cel., n. 158 (Hermann, p. 166): "Francis was greatly consoled by the visitations of God, by which he was made to feel sure that the foun-

dations of his order would always remain unshaken. It was also promised to him that without a doubt the number of those who would fall away would be replaced by the substitution of elect. For once when he was disturbed over bad examples and, thus distressed, gave himself over to prayer, he brought back this rebuke from the Lord: "Why are you disturbed, little man? Did I not place you over my order as its shepherd, and now you do not know that I am its chief protector? I chose you, a simple man, for this task, that what I would do in you to be imitated by the rest they might follow who wished to follow. I have called, I will preserve and feed, and I will choose others to repair the falling away of others, so that if a substitute is not born, I will make him to be born. Do not be disturbed, therefore, but *work out your salvation*, for though the order were reduced to the number of three, it will by my grace remain unshaken."

6. Paul VI, Apostolic Exhortation, November 4, 1965, NCWC, Documentary Service, November 12, 1965, p. 3. This reflects what Pope Paul said sometime before: (*Magno Gaudio Affecti*, May 23, 1964, AAS 56 (1964), p. 567; cf. *TPS* 9, 4 (1963-1964), p. 398. Pope Paul said sometime before: (*Magno Gaudio Affecti*, May 23, 1964, AAS 56 (1964), p. 567; cf. *TPS* 9, 4 (1963-1964), p. 398.

7. Giovanni Battista Cardinal Montini, "Preface," *The Catholic Priesthood*, I, Pierre Veuillot, 2nd. ed., trans. Rev. John A. O'Flynn with Rev. P. Birch and V. Rev. G. Canon Mitchell (Dublin: Gill and Son, 1962), p. xv.

8. Arcadio Cardinal Larraona, "Summary and Farewell," *Religious Community Life in the United States* (Men's Section), (New York: The Paulist Press, 1952), pp. 233-234.

9. Pius XII, *Caritatio Debitum*, November 25, 1948, AAS 40 (1948), p. 551; cf. *The Messenger*, p. 3.

10. Pius XII, *Quemadmodum Tibi*, December 4, 1948, AAS 41 (1949), p. 66; cf. *The Messenger*, p. 44.

11. Paul VI, *Magno Gaudio Affecti*, AAS, p. 569; cf. *TPS*, p. 400.

12. John XXIII, *Questi Primi Mesi*, April 16, 1959, AAS 51 (1959), p. 310; cf. *TPS* 6, 4 (1959-1960), p. 353.

13. Gabriel Buescher O.F.M., "The Renovatio Accomodata," *Franciscan Educational Conference* 37 (1956), pp. 6-7.

14. Cf. *Annuario Pontifico*, 1962 (Citta del Vaticano: Typografia Poliglotta Vaticana, 1962).

15. 1963 National Catholic Almanac, ed. Felician Foy O.F.M. (Paterson: St. Anthony Guild Press, 1963), p. 503.

16. Pius XII, *Annus Sacer,* December 8, 1950, AAS 43 (1951), pp. 33-34; cf. Courtois, p. 182.

17. Ibid., *AAS,* p. 35; cf. Courtois, p. 184.

18. Paul VI, to Clement of Milwaukee O.F.M. Cap. and the General Definitorium O.F.M. Cap., December 17, 1963, *AOFMCap.* 79 (1963), p. 385.

19. Pius XII, *Il Bilancio,* August 3, 1949, *Discorsi e Radio Messaggi di Sua Santita Pio XII,* XI (Citta del Vaticano: Typografia Poliglotta Vaticana, 1950), p. 169; cf. Courtois, pp. 139-140. Unfortunately this is the only statement of a modern pope to Franciscans contained in this collection.

20. Roman Breviary, November 7, lesson 4; Pius XI, *Rite Expiatis,* AAS, p. 166; cf. *RHS,* p. 56.

21. Paul VI, *Ecclesiam Suam,* AAS, p. 632; cf. NCWC, p. 19.

22. Ibid., *AAS,* p. 631; cf. NCWC, p. 18.

23. Valerio Cardinal Valeri, "Sermon at the Opening Pontifical High Mass," *Proceedings of the Second National Congress of Religious of the United States.* (Men's Section), (Notre Dame: University of Notre Dame Press, 1962), pp. 2-3.

24. Giovanni Battista Montini, "Liturgical Formation," (Pastoral Letter, 1958, Lent), approved translation, *Worship,* 33, 3 (1959), pp. 144-145.

25. Suenens, *op. cit.,* p. 117.

26. Giovanni Battista Montini, "Liturgical Formation," *op. cit.,* p. 144.

27. *Ibid.,* p. 141.

28. Pius XII, *Nel Darvi,* July 1, 1956, AAS 48 (1956), p. 576) cf. *RHS,* pp. 74-75.

29. Paul VI, to Augustine Sepinski O.F.M. and the General Definitorium O.F.M., *FHF* 44, 4 (1964), p. 103.

30. Pius XII, *Quemadmodum Tibi,* AAS, p. 66; cf. *The Messenger,* p. 45, p. 44.

31. 2 Cel., n. 70 (Hermann, p. 125; *Words,* p. 215).

32. Pius XII, *Haud Mediocri,* February 11, 1958, AAS 50 (1958), p. 156; cf. *TPS* 5, 2 (1958-1959), p. 204.

33. Paul VI, *Magno Gaudio Affecti,* AAS, pp. 567-568; cf. *TPS,* p. 399.

34. Pius XII, *Caritatis Debitum*, AAS, pp. 551-552; cf. *The Messenger*, p. 3.

35. *Ibid.*, AAS, p. 552; cf. *The Messenger*, p. 3. In a similar vein, Pope Pius XII said to the Capitulars of the Friars Minor (*Postquam Vos*, May 23, 1951, OR 91, 119 [May 24, 1951], p. 1): "Poverty is so necessary, so much in accord with the law of the Gospel, that if a Christian would not at least revere it with affection of the soul and keep his desires free from the slime of earthly ambitions, he would have poor regard for the eternal salvation of his soul. For this reason it is necessary that there be in the Church those who, for the instruction and admonition of others, are pre-eminent in this virtue. You are if you do not depart from your primitive spirit. Therefore, let noble poverty shine forth in your houses and your furnishings and handle earthly things with a sort of reluctance lest you take delight in them. Rather use them moderately as it is said, "He lives well who lives sparsely!'" (Hor. *Od.* 1, II, 16, 13).

36. Cajetan Esser O.F.M. and Engelbert Grau O.F.M., *Love's Reply*, trans. Ignatius Brady O.F.M. (Chicago: Franciscan Herald Press, 1963), pp. 105-106.

37. Pius XII, *Caritatis Debitum*, AAS, p. 551; cf. *The Messenger*, p. 3.

38. Pius XII, *Se l' Umanita*, September 20, 1945, COFMConv., 42 (1945), p. 242; cf. *RHS*, p. 69.

39. *Ibid.*

40. John XXIII, *La Circostanza*, February 27, 1963, AAS 55 (1963), p. 242; cf. *TPS* 9, 2 (1963-1964), p. 144.

41. John XXIII, *Cum Natalicia*, AAS, p. 297; cf. *FHF*, p. 220.

42. Paul VI, at Albano, Italy, August 25, 1963, OR 103, 196 (August 26-27, 1963), p. 1.

43. Pius XII, *Se l' Umanita*, COFMConv., p. 242; cf. *RHS*, p. 69.

44. Suenens, *op. cit.*, p. 58.

45. Pius XI, *Rite Expiatis*, AAS, p. 173; cf. *RHS*, p. 63.

46. Pius XII, *Se l'Umanita*, COFMConv., p. 242; cf. *RHS*, p. 69.

47. Pius XI, *Rite Expiatis*, AAS, p. 161; cf. *RHS*, p. 51.

48. Pius XII, *Caritatis Debitum*, AAS, p. 552; cf. *The Messenger*, p. 3.

49. Giovanni Battista Montini, Address to the Second World Lay Apostolic Congress, October 7, 1957, OR 97, 235 (October 10,

1957), condensed, p. 2; cf. Walsh, p. 20.

50. 2 Cel., n. 148 (Hermann, p. 162; *Words,* p. 178).

51. Esser-Grau, *op. cit.,* pp. 243-244.

52. John XXIII, *Cum Natalicia, AAS,* p. 297; cf. *FHF,* p. 220.

Chapter Six
"THE WORLD HAS URGENT NEED
OF THE FRANCISCAN SPIRIT"

1. John XXIII, *Pacem in Terris,* April 11, 1963, *AAS* 55 (1963), p. 302; cf. *TPS* 9, 1 (1963- 1964), p. 47.

2. Paul VI, *Die Katholikentage,* September 6, 1964, *OR* 104, 207 (September 7-8, 1964), p. 1.

3. Benedict XV, *Gratum Vehementer,* March 7, 1921, *AAS* 13 (1921), pp. 121-122.

4. *Ibid.,* pp. 122-123.

5. Paul VI, *Ecclesiam Suam,* August 6, 1964, *AAS* 56 (1964), p. 648; cf. NCWC, p. 31.

6. John XXIII, *Cum Natalicia,* April 4, 1959, *AAS* 51 (1959), p. 298; cf. *FHF* 38, 7 (1959), pp. 220-221.

7. *LTC,* n. 14 (de Robeck, p. 100; *Words,* p. 172).

8. One of the rare cases wherein a pope talked about our actual vocal preaching to any extent is found in the account of the audience Fr. Clement of Milwaukee O.F.M.Cap. and the General Definitorium O.F.M.Cap. had with Pope Paul VI, December 17, 1963 (*AOFMCap.* 79 [1963], p. 384). In it the pope said: "There are two points which I would like to bring to your attention. The first concerns preaching the word of God — not only insofar as it concerns you Capuchins, but in general. (The second point, acceptance of parishes, will not be discussed here). Our preaching is not geared to modern conditions. Think about it. People today read the newspapers; they think about what they read; they discuss what they read. They listen to the radio; what they hear influences their daily living. They watch television, not only with much interest and pleasure, but also with open minds which also can be impressionable.

Now these same people come to church; they listen to a sermon; and they understand nothing. They go back home without having been aroused or instructed. This means we have to find a new approach. We must study doctrine and explain the eternal truths to them in a way which will be understandable. Unless they understand they will not be able to be saved, for faith comes by hearing. I am not a professor of sacred eloquence and cannot point out the remedy for this problem. But there must be a remedy and we must find it. Take this matter seriously, I beg you, in training and preparing your preachers."

9. Benedict XV, *Sacra Propediem,* January 6, 1921, *AAS* 13 (1921), p. 36; cf. *RHS,* pp. 34-35.

10. Pius XII, *Quemadmodum Tibi,* December 4, 1948, *AAS* 41 (1949), p. 66; cf. *The Messenger,* p. 44.

11. Lk. 12, 49-50.

12. Paul VI, *Il Primo Saluto,* September 1, 1963, *OR* 102, 202 (September 2-3, 1963), p. 1; cf. *TPS* 9, 2 (1963-1964), pp. 176-177.

13. John XXIII, *La Nostra Prima,* June 5, 1960, *AAS* 52 (1960), p. 520; cf. *TPS* 6, 3 (1959-1960), p. 234.

14. John XXIII, *Ad Petri Cathedram,* June 29, 1959, *AAS* 51 (1959), p. 529; cf. *TPS* 5, 4 (1958-1959), p. 382.

15. Pius XI, *Rite Expiatis,* April 30, 1926, *AAS* 18 (1926), p. 169; cf. *RHS,* p. 59.

16. John XXIII, *Questi Primi Mesi,* April 16, 1959, *AAS* 51 (1959), pp. 310-311; cf. *TPS* 6, 4 (1959-1960), p. 353.

17. *Ibid., AAS,* p. 311; cf. *TPS,* pp. 353-354.

18. Leo L. Dubois S.M., *Saint Francis of Assisi, Social Reformer* (New York: Benziger Brothers, 1906), p. 181.

19. Pius XII, *Se l' Umanita,* September 20, 1945, *COFMConv.* 42 (1945), p. 242; cf. *RHS,* p. 68.

20. Romano Guardini, *The Lord,* trans. Elinor Castendyk Briefs (Chicago: Henry Regnery Company, 1954), p. 44.

21. Pius XI, *Con Grande,* July 5, 1928, *AOFMCap.* 44 (1928), p. 191.

22. John XXIII, *Mater et Magistra,* May 15, 1961, *AAS* 53 (1961), p. 440; cf. *TPS* 7, 4 (1960-1961), pp. 325-326.

23. Paul VI, *Magno Gaudio Affecti,* May 23, 1964, *AAS* 56 (1964), p. 568; cf. *TPS* 9, 4 (1963-1964), p. 399.

24. Reminders, 5 (*Words,* p. 133).

25. Louis and Andre Retif, *The Church's Mission in the World,*

trans. Reginald F. Trevett, vol. 102 *Twentieth Century Encyclopedia of Catholicism* (Hawthorn Books, Inc., 70 Fifth Avenue, New York 11, 1962), p. 127.

26. Pius XII, *Quemadmodum Tibi*, AAS, p. 65; cf. *The Messenger*, p. 44.

27. Pius XI, *Divini Redemptoris*, March 19, 1937, AAS 29 (1937), pp. 97-98; cf. Husslein, p. 367.

28. *Ibid.*, AAS, pp. 98-99; cf. Husslein, p. 368.

29. Michael de la Bedoyere, quoting Fernand Tonnet, *The Cardijn Story* (Milwaukee: The Bruce Publishing Company, 1959), p. 47.

30. Pius XII, *Generalis Capituli*, June 5, 1939, *Discorsi e Radiomessaggi di Sua Santita Pio XII* (Milano: Societa Editrice "Vita e Pensiero," 1941), p. 160; cf. *The Third Order Forum* 18, 9 (1939), p. 208.

31. Pius XII, *Quemadmodum Tibi*, AAS, p. 65; cf. *The Messenger*, p. 44.

32. "What Negroes Think of Whites," *Newsweek* 42 (July 29, 1963), p. 32.

33. "A.I.U. Our Instrument for Interracial Peace," *FHF* 42, 2 (1963), p. 49.

34. Benedict XV, *Sacra Propediem*, AAS, pp. 36-37; cf. *RHS*, pp. 34-35.

35. Leo XIII, to the tertiaries of Assisi, March 22, 1878, Peruffo, p. 81.

36. Pius X, St., *La Principale Gloria*, May 5, 1909, Peruffo p. 271.

37. Paul VI, *Il Primo Saluto*, OR, p. 1; cf. *TPS*, p. 177.

38. John XXIII, to the tertiaries of Italy, July 2, 1961, *OR* 101, 153 (July 5, 1961), p. 1.

39. Pius XII, *Nel Darvi*, July 1, 1956, AAS 48 (1956), p. 574; cf. *RHS*, p. 72.

40. Leo XIII, *Auspicato*, September 17, 1882, ASS 15 (1882), p. 150; cf. *RHS*, pp. 17-18.

41. Pius X, St., *Tertium Franciscalium*, September 8, 1912, AAS 4 (1912), p. 584; cf. *RHS*, p. 28.

42. Benedict XV, *Sacra Propediem*, AAS, p. 36; cf. *RHS*, p. 34.

43. de la Bedoyere, quoting Msgr. Cardijn, *op. cit.*, p. 60.

44. Pius XII, *Nel Darvi*, AAS, p. 575; cf. *RHS*, p. 73.

45. Pius XI, *Rite Expiatis*, AAS, p. 174; cf. *RHS*, p. 64.

46. Pius XI, to Leonard Bello O.F.M., quoted in *Third Order Forum* 18, 4 (1939), p. 96.

47. "Responsibility for the Third Order," Four Ministers General, September 17, 1951, *AOFMCap.* 67 (1951), p. 207; cf. *The Franciscan Vision of Life,* (Chicago: Franciscan Herald Press, 1957), p. 23.

48. John XXIII, to the tertiaries of Italy, July 2, 1961, *OR* 101, 153 (July 5, 1961), p. 1.

49. *Ibid.,*

50. Benedict XV, *Sacra Propediem, AAS,* pp. 39-40; cf. *RHS,* pp. 37-38.

51. Paul VI, *Ecclesiam Suam, AAS,* p. 649; cf. NCWC, p. 32.

52. Pius XII, *Nel Darvi, AAS,* p. 577; cf. *RHS,* p. 76.

53. Pius XI, to the tertiaries of Lombardy, September 15, 1925, Peruffo, p. 396.

54. Pius XII, *Nel Darvi, AAS,* p. 574; cf. *RHS,* p. 72.

55. Pius XII, *Se l' Umanita, COFMConv.,* p. 243; cf. *RHS,* p. 70.

56. Pius XII, *Nel Darvi, AAS,* p. 577; cf. *RHS,* p. 75.

57. John XXIII, *Questi Primi Mesi, AAS,* p. 313; cf. *TPS,* p. 355.

Index